Plague, Flood and Gewgaws; Wisbech and the Fens in Tudor and Stuart Times

By

Diane Calton Smith

To Jan and Tony,
present day residents
of Guyhirn!

Diane
13-8-19.

Published by New Generation Publishing in 2019

Copyright © Diane Calton Smith 2019

First Edition

The author asserts the moral right under the Copyright, Designs and Patents Act 1988 to be identified as the author of this work.

All Rights reserved. No part of this publication may be reproduced, stored in a retrieval system or transmitted, in any form or by any means without the prior consent of the author, nor be otherwise circulated in any form of binding or cover other than that which it is published and without a similar condition being imposed on the subsequent purchaser.

www.newgeneration-publishing.com

 New Generation Publishing

For Tony,
an honorary Fen Tiger.
And to all tigers everywhere.

Front cover image shows detail from a painting in Peckover House depicting King's Hall, North Brink, Wisbech (with permission of the National Trust Photo Library).

Also by Diane Calton Smith:

Fenland Histories:
A Georgian House on the Brink (2015)
(Winner of a Cambridgeshire Association for Local History [CALH] award)
Webbed Feet and Wildfowlers (2017)

Fenland Mysteries:
Quiet While Dollie Sings (2016)
The Quayside Poet (2018)

CONTENTS

FOREWORD 1

CHAPTER ONE: Collapse; The Times of Henry VII 5

CHAPTER TWO: A Supreme Head; The Times of Henry VIII 25

CHAPTER THREE: Chop and Change; The Times of Edward VI and Mary I 46

CHAPTER FOUR: Prison, Plague and Gewgaws; The Times of Elizabeth I 58

    A Little Care in the Community 70

    Plague 73

    Goings-On at the Castle 83

CHAPTER FIVE: 'Vast and Queachy Soyle'; James I and Charles I 97

    Purity and Charity 107

    The Matter of the Fens 110

CHAPTER SIX: The Dry Land Smiles; The Protectorate 122

CHAPTER SEVEN: 'A Base Unwholesome Air'; Charles II and the Last Stuarts 140

    Refuge in Wisbech 154

CHAPTER EIGHT: Doublets and Chamber Pots; The Way They Lived ....
.... 164

    From Shutter to Sash; Where They Lived 164

    Headroom for Big Wigs: Travel 175

    Pottage and Ale; Food and Drink 178

Abracadabra; Health and Hygiene 187

Red Heels and Farthingales; What They Wore .. 195

Dawn to Sunset; Work 209

Spinning Tops...and Bottoms; Play Time 217

A Headless Man on the Moon; Thinking and Learning 228

The Doffing of Caps; Social Graces and Society 237

AFTERWORD AND THANKS 246

APPENDIX 248

BIBLIOGRAPHY 249

INDEX OF NAMES AND PLACES (except Wisbech itself) 251

FOREWORD

Wisbech and the Fenland around it could already boast quite an eventful history by the end of the medieval period. The people who lived there could look back on invasion, flood, famine and plague and know that somehow they had survived it all.

But now there was a new king on the English throne, one who would bring a new age and start a new dynasty. Henry VII was the first of the Tudors, a king who would introduce an era of huge change and decades of upheaval. The way ordinary people behaved, prayed, even the way they were expected to think, would be overturned.

From the dawning of the Tudor age to that of the Georgians, 'Plague, Flood and Gewgaws' follows the progress of the Fenlanders through two hundred turbulent years. It traces the evolution of their world from a medieval landscape, alive with the sound of monastery bells, to being a part of Great Britain.

As is usual when writing about such distant times, many old terms crop up and where possible I have added explanations in brackets. All references to money, of course, are pre-decimal, so for anyone youthful enough to be unfamiliar with pounds, shillings and old pence, I have added a brief appendix.

Following the progress of Wisbech and the Fens through such a long stretch of time is also bound to unearth a few mysteries. I was recently giving a talk to a group of Wisbech ladies when two of them told me about the curious wording of their house deeds. Their homes in Willow Way sit close to the eastern side of the A1101 dual carriageway as it passes through town, roughly following the course of the old Well Stream. When these ladies bought their houses in 1971 they were made aware of a clause in their deeds which allowed monks access to the wells on their land! Apparently, there is evidence of an old well in each of their gardens and the ladies asked me where the monks were likely to have come from in the past.

This curious question set me thinking, because it's a bit of a conundrum. Before the dissolution of the monasteries, the monks could have come from either the Hospital of St John the Baptist, thought to have been situated between North Brink and Dowgate in Leverington, or the leper hospital between Elm and Wisbech.

However, in those days the Well Stream formed the boundary between the Wisbech Hundred to the west and the Leet of Marshland to the east. Willow Way, therefore, would have been outside the Wisbech boundary. Would monks from the Wisbech Hundred have needed access to wells in Marshland, on the other side of the river?

As was usual with religious houses, it is likely that the leper hospital between Elm and Wisbech, the closest location to the modern houses, was endowed with land. If so, some of that land may well have been on the far side of the river and the hospital monks may have needed access to it, even if the land was leased out. This, of course, is only a theory. It remains a mystery and I hope that one day the answer will emerge. I mention it here as an example of some of the fascinating riddles which continue to present themselves.

Not everyone finds the area so inspiring. In around 1909, a man signing himself simply as LG sent an essay about the Fens to a magazine called 'Fenland Notes and Queries'. In it he described the uninterrupted view across the Fens and summarised it as the 'joyless grey of Fen landscape'. His conclusion included the words, 'the Fenland does not yet claim a historian. Few would buy his book.'

I suppose I should thank him for the warning!

Whatever the opinion of a disenchanted Edwardian, the Fens with their boundless layers of history and tradition are loved by many. And it is the ordinary folk who farmed, laboured, prayed, drained and rebelled who fascinate me the most. It is these people this book is about. It isn't the masters who occupy centre stage here, but the people who had little choice but to do as they were told.

Oh, and it's about the Fen Tigers too, the ones who refused to behave.

The Fen Tigers, past and present, are part of the life blood of the Fens. It is to them that I dedicate this book.

Ely Cathedral

CHAPTER ONE

Collapse; The Times of Henry VII

It must truly have been a night to remember, when the old church tower fell down.

Even above the sounds of the storm, the noise of collapsing masonry, as heavy stone crashed through the roof of the church nave, must have been deafening. As the tower crumbled and collapsed, it fell diagonally through the roof of the nave, destroying a mighty row of Norman columns. Those huge columns, which had supported the roof since the year 1111, were reduced to rubble.

The sound of such destruction, however bad the weather, would have carried throughout the small Fenland town of Wisbech, vibrations shaking the ground and bringing people from their beds. Townsfolk would have come running to find out what was happening. What confronted them must have looked like a modern bomb site, the ruin of something which until that moment must have seemed indestructible.

At a time when the Church was central to all aspects of life, the fall of this apparently solid and reliable symbol of their faith is bound to have been terrifying.

Among the first to arrive at the scene were likely to have been members of the Guild of the Holy Trinity, the guildsmen who practically ran the town. The alderman, the principal guild official, must have had to wait until morning to assess the full extent of the damage. It wouldn't have taken him long, though, to understand how bad things were. It was going to take many years and huge sums of money to save the parish church of St Peter and St Paul.

The people of Wisbech who witnessed this devastation were no strangers to bad news. Ferocious storms were nothing new either. In earlier times, when the coastline had reached further inland and Wisbech had been by the sea, waves had battered the sea walls so powerfully on many occasions that they had been broken down. Heavy rainfall had added to the problem, bursting river banks and flooding the town and countryside time and time again.

And now, at the beginning of the Tudor age, the weather was growing colder. The British Isles were entering a mini ice age and there would be no relief from this freeze for the next three hundred years or more.

The Black Death that had blighted the country in the fourteenth century had reduced the population of England and Wales by more than a third, to between two and a half and three million. Some villages had been abandoned entirely and in Wisbech around a tenth of the homes and workshops had been left without tenants. A great number of livestock had also been wiped out by disease. This meant poverty for many people, exacerbated by harsh winters and continuous wet summers that led to crop failure.

Yet the people of the Fens had survived. They had always been good fishermen and wildfowlers, skilled in making the most of the untamed, unpredictable and largely waterlogged Fens that surrounded them. Because of this, they were perhaps better able to cope than most.

But what was early Tudor Wisbech like? At the time the church tower collapsed in around 1500, what did the town consist of?

For a start, it was no longer on the coast. Ever since William the Conqueror had built his castle in Wisbech to keep an eye on the coastline, the estuary had slowly been silting up and changing the nature of the landscape. The silt, carried downstream by the rivers, had played its part in the creation of a marsh where the estuary had been. Crabbe Marsh now separated the town from the sea.

Wisbech was part of the administrative area known as the Wisbech Hundred. The Hundred, its eastern border defined by the Well Stream, extended as far north as Tydd St Giles, to Upwell in the south and Guyhirn in the west.

The main river running through town was the Nene, but it had not always been so. Until the thirteenth century, the Well Stream had flowed through Wisbech to the sea, connecting the town with the Rivers Nene and Ouse at Outwell. However, because the Well Stream had become so choked with silt, new channels had been cut around 1250. This work had eased navigation but diverted Wisbech's old river trade to King's Lynn. For more than two hundred years, Wisbech had managed without an efficient river link with the rest of the country. Then finally, in the 1480s, Bishop Morton of Ely had come to the rescue, constructing Morton's Leam between Stanground and Guyhirn. This new channel joined the old Wysbeck River at Guyhirn and directed a new course of the Nene through Wisbech.

Wisbech's replenished river was already bringing prosperity to the town. The old Well Stream remained too, though its problems with silt further upstream made it impassable to river traffic for months at a time. Following roughly the line of today's A1101 dual carriageway, it joined the Nene to the north of the town.

During periods of prosperity, Wisbech had expanded northwards to fill the angle formed by the confluence of the two rivers. To the south, the town reached as far as the Timber Market, which hugged the bank of the old Well Stream, close to modern day Norfolk Street. Though the town's eastern side butted up against the river bank and could expand no further that way, it spread gradually westwards along the Nene in the Guyhirn direction.

At the heart of the town was the castle. Rebuilt as an ecclesiastical palace between 1478 and 1483 by the same Bishop Morton of Ely, the new palace was of red brick with windows of stained glass. Still known as Wisbech Castle, it must have been both handsome and awe inspiring. According to William Weston, a prisoner of the castle in later times, the central keep was built on a mound within high, strong walls and was protected by both an inner and an outer moat, or dyke, as it was usually called.

The new castle shared a multitude of functions with its Norman predecessor. Since early times, it had been in the charge of the Constable of the Castle and had served as the bishop's residence whenever he visited Wisbech. It was also the region's administration centre and housed law courts and a gaol. Court hearings took place in the castle's mote hall, located in the area now called Castle Square.

Meetings of the Commission of Sewers, the body responsible for local drainage, were also held there.

The law courts, known as assizes, with their judge (the justice of assize) and jury of twelve men, dealt with the most serious crimes, such as treason and murder. These hearings had been held in the mote hall since the 1100s, when Wisbech had first become an assize town. Sittings were held twice a year. The accused due to be tried were brought into town by boat and held in the castle gaol for up to six months, pending the next assizes. Security, though tight, was not entirely foolproof. In 1492 Sir Thomas Hobard, the Constable of the Castle, was fined the significant sum of five pounds when prisoners managed to escape from his gaol.

Less serious crimes were also dealt with in the mote hall, but at the Quarter Sessions which were held four times a year, at Epiphany, Easter, Midsummer and Michaelmas. Quarter Sessions were presided over by a chairman with at least two Justices of the Peace and a jury. For more trivial crimes, there were sittings of the Hundred Courts, also held in the mote hall.

There was, of course, no police force in Tudor times. Instead, the region was overseen by the king's representative, the High Sheriff. He was responsible for peace keeping in the whole of the Isle of Ely and for keeping an eye on the legal process and law court procedures.

Criminal trials usually resulted from accusations brought by the victims of crimes to the local Justices of the Peace. The town constable, usually a part time role for a local man, made the arrest and took the accused to the castle gaol, where he or she would be held until the next Quarter Session. If the Quarter Session justices considered the crime serious enough, the accused could be referred to the next assizes.

Since before the Norman invasion, most of the land in the Manor of Wisbech, as the town and land around it were still called, had belonged to the Church. Although much of this land had been rented out, the Bishop of Ely still held overall responsibility for the manor, and one of a new bishop's first tasks on entering office was the appointment of a legal team. When Bishop Alcock succeeded Bishop Morton in 1486 he appointed Justices of Assize (judges) for the Isle of Ely and Commissioners of Gaols for Ely and Wisbech. Their names, as recorded in the bishop's register, were Sir William Huse, John Brewode, Robert Bradbury, John Burgoyn and Robert Spencer.

The castle's brick built gatehouse overlooked an open forecourt leading to the town bridge, close to where Clarkson's Memorial stands today.

The area between the wooden town bridge and the far side of the market place had for centuries been known as the New Market. This was the main commercial area of town. Between the outer castle dyke and the market place were rows of narrow burgage (or burgess) plots. These strips of land were occupied by shops and workshops where blacksmiths, chandlers, carpenters, coopers and many other craftsmen laboured away. More than forty tradesmen are thought to have been working there at the time.

On both sides of the road later to be known as High Street were dozens more burgage plots. The buildings squeezed on to these long, narrow plots usually had a shop at the front, facing the street, and outbuildings that stretched behind. The plots on the western side of the street backed on to the river.

Around the market place were more narrow fronted shops selling all manner of goods. There were also a good many inns, one of which was the Bull, another the Horn and Pheasant (or the Horn). Originally called the Swan, it could trace its origins back to before 1435 and would eventually become the Rose and Crown we know today.

The shops and other buildings around the market place were mostly of late medieval construction, typically two or three storeys high with each storey projecting slightly over the one below. Generally, the shop faced on to the market place and goods were displayed on trestles outside. The shopkeeper and his family usually lived upstairs.

The whole square, with its hostelries, shops and workshops, must have been alive with activity and noise, especially on Saturdays when the weekly market was held, but it must also have been a trifle malodorous. Open drains (or sewers) ran through the market place and along some streets, carrying waste of every kind into the river.

The town streets, as in the rest of the country, were poorly surfaced, dusty when dry and muddy when wet. In 1497 Andreas Franciscus, a Venetian visitor to London, expressed his distaste for the state of the city's streets. Perhaps more accustomed to the drier conditions of his own country, he found it appalling how quickly the rain turned streets into seas of evil smelling mud. The smell would not have been improved by the rubbish left to decay in the sewers. Though his comments were about London, Wisbech can hardly have been any better.

Behind the market place, on the opposite side from the castle, ran Ship Lane (modern day Hill Street). The guild hall is believed to have been situated there.

The oldest building in Wisbech was the parish church of St Peter and St Paul. Dating from 1111, it was nestled between the castle dyke and the Well Stream. In the early 1500s, of course, it was undergoing major reconstruction following the collapse of its Norman tower. The old tower had been built at the western end of the building, rather too close perhaps to the castle dyke. Centuries of flooding and subsidence must seriously have weakened its foundations, ultimately causing its destruction.

Leading from the church, and following the line of the castle dyke, was Deadman's Lane. It curved round, roughly where Love Lane and Alexandra Road are now, towards the town bridge.

On the other side of the wooden bridge was the area known as the Old Market. This is believed to have been the site of the original Saxon hamlet of Wisbech. The label 'old' simply defined it as separate from the 'new market' district across the river. The Old Market had become something of a dormitory town by the early 1500s, but still had its own supply of workshops and warehouses which filled the narrow plots going down to the river.

Behind the Old Market, leading out of town towards Leverington, was open farm land; the cultivated fields of Sandyland.

The northern bank of the Nene, later to be known as North Brink, was divided into more burgage plots. These were sparsely occupied, it is thought, by dwellings, warehouses, barns and other farm buildings. In 2015, during gardening work at the National Trust's Peckover House, the remains of a brick wall were discovered. Experts were called in who decided that the wall, which ran in a straight line from the river direction, dated from the early Tudor period. It is believed to have been a dividing wall between two burgage plots.

Remains of an early Tudor wall discovered at Peckover House in 2015 (with permission of the National Trust)

On the opposite side of town, on the bank of the Well Stream and close to modern day Norfolk Street, was the Timber Market. Though the river further upstream was badly silted up and sluggish, this part of the river, which was close to the tidal entrance from the Wash, would still have been navigable. The Timber Market was a thriving industrial area. Lay Subsidy Records, which were used to assess townspeople for tax, showed shipwrights, butchers, blacksmiths and carpenters working there. Barnack stone, as well as timber, was brought to the quayside there on Fen lighters (barges) to supply the local building industry.

Some of the names mentioned in the records are interesting. For example, William Merkaunt is listed as a merchant working in the Timber Market. His surname indicates a long family tradition of trading as merchants or 'merkaunt's.

Beyond the furthest reaches of the town were villages and hamlets which had seen little change for centuries. The manors of Elm, Leverington, Tydd St Giles, Tydd St Mary and Newton in the Isle had been referred to since early times in local records.

Villages such as Emneth, Gorefield and Parson Drove had begun as hamlets attached to their neighbouring manors, but had later become parishes in their own right. Emneth, though originally a hamlet of Elm, had grown so rapidly by the 1400s that the smaller manors of Haybech and Inglethorpe had grown up within its boundaries.

Ecclesiastical records surviving from the times contain some interesting snippets of information about life in these smaller manors.

In 1488, for example, an agreement was recorded between the Rector of Elm and the Vicar of Emneth about the tithes due to each of them on locally grown crops. The produce listed in the record shows an interesting variety of food being grown. Wheat, barley, oats and rye were grown in plenty, to satisfy the constant demand for bread. The vegetables listed included beans, peas, turnips, garlic, onions, mustard and leeks. Flax, used to make linseed oil and linen, and hemp to produce rope, were also grown in great quantities.

The record also mentioned produce harvested from the Fen on which tithes were due. Reeds, osiers, straw and agistments (permission for an individual to graze his animals on private land for a fee), as well as wild birds such as herons, bitterns, cranes, and ducks, were all listed. Tithes were also payable on coppiced wood, willows and faggots.

Whether people lived in towns or villages, the fear of flooding never went away. Since the thirteenth century, the Commission of Sewers had been responsible for the maintenance of local sea and river defences. With the king's authority, they ordered whatever work they considered necessary to be done. In the Manorial Court Rolls of Elm of 1503 it was recorded that the inhabitants of Friday Bridge were ordered to clean and repair all the ditches and banks in their vicinity. Another ruling at around the same time stated that the inhabitants of March could neither fish nor gather reeds in the Wisbech Hundred. Anyone caught doing so was to be fined three shillings and four pence, a serious amount for the times.

Much of the commission's work concerned the waterways which were of huge importance, both to navigation and drainage. The constant build-up of silt in the rivers was one of the commission's main challenges and waterways frequently had to be scoured out to restore the flow.

Surviving detail from the Town Book of Wisbech shows that the inhabitants of the Wisbech Hundred were responsible for scouring and cleansing Morton's Leam between Wisbech and 'Mid Fen Tree'. This rather vague landmark is thought to have been half way between Eldernell, near Whittlesey, and Guyhirn.

Although this ruling and others of its kind were necessary, they were met with a lot of complaint because they required people to travel out of town to do the work. They still thought parochially, concerned only with the section of ditch or river bank close to their own homes. Few would have denied, though, that Morton's Leam had improved the local economy. As well as aiding navigation, its role as a drainage channel for fields was helping to improve local crop production.

Before the leam had been constructed, the River Nene between Peterborough and March had consisted of a number of meandering streams. Heavily loaded lighters (barges) had travelled south along the old course from Peterborough, through Whittlesey, Ramsey and March to Outwell, and the going had been difficult, to say the least. Low levels of water in the river at certain times of the year had caused boats to be held up for weeks on Whittlesey or Ramsey Meres. Very often, they'd had to wait until autumn rain refilled the river and allowed them to continue their journey. Now at last, using Morton's Leam, they could travel with relative ease all the way from Wansford to Wisbech along the new course of the Nene.

There had been improvements in other respects too.

By the end of the 1400s, the feudal system had finally come to an end. There had been several contributing factors, among them the sharp fall in population due to the Black Death and Wars of the Roses. Any remaining tied peasants may have served in their feudal lords' army during the war years and the survivors are unlikely to have returned to lives of servitude on the old manors.

Land owners found themselves with too few peasants to do the work and were obliged to pay more to fill the vacancies. At last, the working classes had stronger bargaining powers. They were able to demand better pay and conditions and the old shackles could no longer hold them.

The loss of cheap labour, once so freely available under the feudal system, made old manorial land less profitable. Much of this demesne land (acreage owned by the manorial lord and farmed for him by his tied peasants) was therefore sold off or rented out.

The Bishop of Ely was one such manorial lord. He had begun to sell and let unprofitable land in the Isle of Ely and in 1429 the last parcel of demesne land in the Wisbech Hundred had been leased out. Local business minded men had made the most of this once-in-a-lifetime opportunity, buying as much land as they could. Thomas Barowe of Tydd, for example, had acquired forty-six and a half acres, and Hamlet Norbury of Wisbech a hundred and forty-two and a half acres of land around Wisbech and in Leverington.

The bishop's role had largely changed from estate management to rent collection. As time went by, he needed to spend less time on his manors and it became sensible to delegate some of his work. In Wisbech, these tasks fell to the Guild of the Holy Trinity, the highly esteemed religious brotherhood which already ran most of the town's affairs.

But the people of Wisbech were probably more concerned about the ruined church at the centre of their community. If the more superstitious among them saw the calamity as an omen, they may have had a point. Later generations may well have looked back on the incident as a warning of the turmoil to come.

Church attendance on Sundays was compulsory. Very little information survives to give any clues about how the obligatory church attendance was managed without a functional parish church. Local chapels and neighbouring parishes perhaps helped out, but we can only guess.

The restoration of St Peter and St Paul's Church, quite apart from the raising of funds with which to do it, was a huge task. The collapse of the tower on to the nave and the destruction of a whole arcade of columns meant major and prolonged rebuilding work. Whatever temporary provisions were made for church attendance had to continue for several years. The entire project, including a new tower, would take decades to complete.

Meanwhile, the Guild of the Holy Trinity busied itself with running the town. It was the most prominent of the town's guilds and since its founding in 1379, had become very wealthy. Numerous endowments of land had been made to the guild over the years, boosting its rental income and status. The guild's principal officer and the town's most important man was the alderman. Its other officers were the dean, two skyvens (stewards), a scribe, two store keepers, a server and a bailiff, who by 1475 was paid £1.6s.8d a year. There was also a keeper of the jewels.

The role of the keeper of the jewels was a very important one. As well as land, the guild received other valuable gifts which had to be kept securely. Even in its early years, the guild listed amongst its possessions a silver gilt cross, a pair of coral beads, a pair of amber beads, three pairs of jet beads, crucifixes of silver and an image of the Virgin Mary. These treasures were kept in a strongbox requiring four keys to open it. One was held by the alderman, one by the vicar, one by the keeper of the jewels and the fourth by another trusted guild member.

It was quite usual for the vicar to be enrolled into the guild. In 1503 Richard Wyatt, the vicar of Wisbech, paid six shillings and eight pence on being admitted to the guild.

Incidentally, the role of vicar at St Peter and St Paul's had recently acquired new status. Usually, a vicar only ran a church on behalf of a rector, but in 1479 the incumbent had been named as perpetual vicar of Wisbech. This meant that he lived permanently in the parish to carry out his duties.

It was usual for wealthy people to leave money to the Church and other religious institutions. Such legacies often accompanied requests for prayers to be said for their souls after death in the hope that the afterlife might be made more bearable. This hope brought a lot of wealth to the Church.

The Guild of the Holy Trinity also did well out of these fears and beliefs. Among the many legacies it received was one from John Thurston, a chaplain of Wisbech. In his Will of the fourth of February 1497, he bequeathed a vestment to the guild and a chalice for the altar of St Katherine. Another citizen, Reginald Gyles, in his Will of the twenty-second of November 1494, left money for candles on nine altars, as well as forty acres of land to the guild.

By all accounts, the guild was run in a disciplined manner and looked after the town well. The brethren had set times for prayers, or at least for some of them. The first of the day were at 6am, the second at 8am and the third were to be fitted in when convenient!

One of their rulings shows the lawlessness of the times and how much fear and suspicion there was. In 1481 it was ruled that no foreigners should be admitted to the guild without the full permission of the members. By 'foreigners', they meant strangers. During such violent times, it made sense to be wary of outsiders, and men with the means to do so usually carried swords. Priests were no exception. It wasn't uncommon for churches and churchyards to be the scenes of murder and violent struggles.

The guilds were renowned for their acts of charity. Among the most notable good deeds of the Guild of the Holy Trinity were the building of almshouses in 1476 and the earlier founding of the grammar school.

The 'Schola Sanctae Trinitatis de Wysbech' had been founded by the guild in 1379. The small room above the south porch of St Peter and St Paul's Church had always served as the classroom. In 1506 it was decided that the schoolmaster should be paid 'from Midsummer next eight marks sterling' per annum (about £5.40) in wages. Though the porch and school room may have suffered damage when the tower collapsed, that part of the building must have been made useable by this date, in order for lessons to continue.

It would have been helpful to the parish if the porch had survived the worst of the damage. Church porches were used at that time for far more than just shelter from bad weather. It was usual for Christenings and weddings to take place there, rather than in the main body of the church, even though they must have been draughty and damp affairs for much of the year.

The guild's considerable land holdings had to be actively managed. A lot of the land was let out and rent duly collected. As examples of this, in 1515 the guild granted a lease on seven acres of land with fishing rights in Newton for ten years at ten percent per annum. Another ten acres of pasture in Fenland Field were let for twenty years at ten shillings a year and four guildsmen had to ride over regularly to oversee the property. The guild's land was clearly spread over quite a wide area.

Beyond the reaches of the town, farms and villages stretched the seemingly limitless open Fen. Despite man's occasional intervention, water had always had the last word, rising and falling with the seasons and dominating the marshy land. The Fens were unpredictable and treacherous for anyone who didn't understand their ways.

Fen ague (malaria) was rife, transmitted by the mosquitoes that thrived in pools of stagnant water. Although Fen people had become largely immune to this disease, few could escape the rheumatism and arthritis caused by the constant damp. Even children were crippled by it and the middle aged were often bent over by its effects. Some pain relief came from the opium extracted from white poppies growing in the Fens. This drug had been used since early times to numb pain and its help must have been very welcome to people whose lives were invariably hard and short.

Although Fenland life was harsh, there were some benefits. Apart from the abundance of fish, eels and water fowl for the table, geese and ducks provided meat, eggs and feathers. Fenmen, despite their troubles, often slept on mattresses stuffed with feathers. Willow saplings and reeds could be harvested as building materials and peat was cut for winter fires.

Travel across the Fens brought its own challenges. Pathways crossing the wide stretches of marsh were perilous and had to be precisely navigated. There were areas where even the most experienced Fenmen would not venture. Punts were used to cross flooded marshland and lighters carried heavy loads along the waterways. The lighters were generally pulled along by a horse or a boy on the bank. In places where the tow path came to an end on one bank and switched to the opposite side, the horse or boy had to swim across the river so that the journey could continue. Childhood was short and tough for many.

For centuries, stilts had been used for walking across difficult terrain. The sound of Fenmen making their way through sucking mud and water, whether on stilts or on foot, earned them the name of 'slodgers'.

In winter, the flat, frozen landscape was ideal for skating. Early skates were very primitive, made of animal bones strapped to boots, and it wouldn't be until the seventeenth century that iron skate blades arrived from Holland. Even so, Fenlanders skated for miles along frozen rivers and across the open Fen. In later times they would become famous for it.

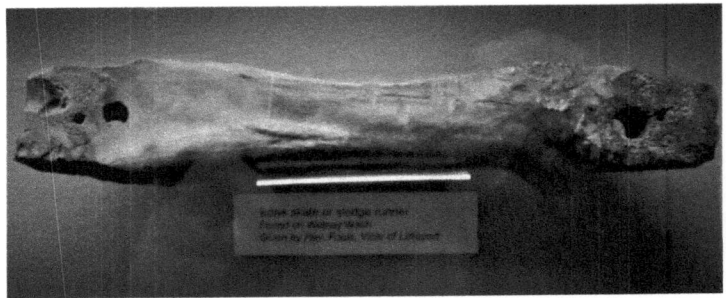

Early bone skate on display at Wisbech and Fenland Museum (with permission of the museum)

With very little communication with other parts of the country, it probably made no difference to the Fenmen which king occupied the throne, so long as they were left in peace. Henry VII would not have worried them a great deal. He was hard working and careful, seen by many as dour and grasping, and it was the gentry who suffered from his heavy fines and taxes. Fenlanders wouldn't have lost a lot of sleep over that.

The king's influence would have been felt only in small ways. Kings had always controlled the ownership of swans, keeping most of them for their own tables. Permission to keep these precious birds was sparingly given. Royally appointed officers called keepers of swans marked the beaks of the birds in their care to reduce the likelihood of theft. An Act of 1482 had prohibited anyone from using their own swan marks, unless they owned freehold land worth five marks (about £3.35) annually.

The swans on Whittlesey Mere belonged to the crown and were carefully tended. In 1468 the swan herd, Richard Forster, had been obliged to investigate reports of local folk catching cygnets with hooks and nets. No doubt that practice was swiftly brought to an end! In 1507 Henry VII granted the office of keeper of the swanery on the mere to David Cecil for seven years.

Whittlesey Mere was one of the largest fresh water lakes in southern Britain. Measuring about three miles in width and six in length, it was a rich source of pike, perch, carp, tench, eels, roach and of course swans. As a resource, the mere had always been greatly valued, mentioned as early as the seventh century in a charter held by Medehamstede (Peterborough) Abbey. The mere, like the smaller Ugg Mere and Ramsey Mere, formed part of the watery landscape of the Fens and brought benefits for many.

Though times were undoubtedly hard, there was at least some provision for the poor. The monasteries had always considered charity a religious duty and most of them had an infirmary for the care of the sick. Alms were given to the poor, and travellers were provided with food and shelter. To support this charity, a proportion of the tithes from parish churches was paid to the monasteries. The Fenland abbeys of Ely, Ramsey, Thorney, Crowland and Peterborough supported the community in this way.

Where there was no monastic infirmary nearby, towns sometimes had a hospital of their own. There had once been one in Wisbech, dedicated to St John the Baptist and thought to have been situated between the north bank of the Nene and Dowgate in Leverington. Unfortunately, it had closed around the end of the 1300s.

Parish churches were also responsible for giving alms to the poor. Usually, a quarter of their tithes were set aside for this purpose, but attitudes were not always helpful. Late medieval opinion had declared poverty to be the product of sin, a belief which had made things even harder for life's least fortunate. By the early 1500s, though, there was some softening of this attitude.

The records kept by the Guild of the Holy Trinity make several references to their care for the needy. One example concerns their 1506 Trinity Sunday feast in the guildhall when the steward served the poor at a separate table with leftover meat.

News of the death of Henry VII in 1509 does not seem to have been greeted with excessive mourning and gnashing of teeth. His rather straight-faced reign had brought stability after the devastation of the Wars of the Roses, but the feasting and dancing which marked his passing in some regions suggests that his efforts were not entirely appreciated.

It was time for another Henry.

'New' arcade of columns in St Peter's Church following the collapse of the Norman tower (with permission of the parish church)

CHAPTER TWO

A Supreme Head; The Times of Henry VIII

Henry VIII was barely eighteen years of age when he came to the throne, bringing with him a zest for life and a love of music, dance, hunting and jousting. How much the people of Wisbech and the Fens joined in with the national rejoicing that marked his coronation can only be guessed at, but it is likely that they felt a degree of optimism at the thought of a new era.

The population of Wisbech was still small. Lay Subsidy records from 1524 to 1525 show 1,764 people living in the town, with a mere 434 in Elm and 336 in Upwell. Villages on the other side of town were a little more populous, Leverington having 763 residents, Tydd St Giles 546 and Newton in the Isle 441.

The townsfolk of Wisbech, though few in number, were getting on well with the rebuilding of their church. The remains of the broken tower and fallen masonry from the nave had been cleared away and a renovated building was rising from the rubble. The damaged southern row of columns had been replaced by a graceful new arcade. Rather than replicating the heavy Norman architecture of the originals, the new columns had been constructed in the elegant Perpendicular style. A row of clerestory windows had been installed in both the northern and southern sides, letting more light into the church and giving it a feeling of spaciousness.

An arcade of original Norman columns remained on the northern side and no one seemed to mind that the two rows no longer matched. The two contrasting styles remain today as a reminder of the church's long and interesting past.

The newly rebuilt St Peter's still lacked a tower, however. Its construction was having to be carefully planned and the necessary funds raised to build it.

At around this time, the Guild of the Holy Trinity constructed a chapel of its own. Though the chapel adjoined the chancel on the south-east corner of the parish church, there was no connecting door between the two buildings. The chapel functioned as a separate place of worship, its large windows letting in plenty of light and lending the structure all the beauty and elegance of the latest style. Outside, its stone was extensively carved with coats of arms and the distinct form of the Tudor rose. Displayed like a row of badges, the chapel's carved roses proclaimed the guild's allegiance to the Tudors who would ultimately bring about its downfall.

Tudor Rose stone carving on the exterior of the Guild of the Holy Trinity's chapel, St Peter's Church

Local people contributed generously to the new tower fund. Robert Smith in his Will of 1520 left twenty pounds 'for the building of the new steeple' and in 1525 'Moris Byrde of Wysbyche' left ten shillings to the same cause. The Guild of the Holy Trinity also chipped in, donating £2.3s.4d in 1524.

The construction of the tower took a long time. Even by 1538 the alderman of the guild was still assigning money to the project, contributing a further four pounds.

At last, the new tower was completed. Built on the north-west corner of the church, it was slightly detached from the main building to prevent further damage to the nave in the event of another collapse. Its new location was well away, though, from the unstable ground close to the castle dyke on the western side, where the old structure had stood. Like the guild's chapel, the tower was richly embellished with coats of arms and rose in all its glory to herald a new era.

One of the coats of arms was that of Bishop Goodrich, the new Bishop of Ely from 1534. In accordance with tradition, the town of Wisbech had presented him with a purse containing £7.6s.8d on his first coming to the See of Ely.

Once the church was completed, the Guild of the Holy Trinity was able to turn more of its attention to the running of the town. By 1521 the guild had become so wealthy and influential that a larger team of officials was needed to manage its affairs. As well as the alderman and dean, there was now a clerk, a steward, two cupbearers, two servers, two chamberlains, a bailiff and a door porter. Rich individuals continued to bequeath land to the guild, which now owned a hundred and eighty-seven acres. The land was spread over a considerable area, some to the north of the town and forty acres in Meadowgate Lane and Emneth.

Practically all of it was leased out and, under the guild's rules, no one could sell their lease without the consent of the alderman and twelve of the brethren.

Guild members demanded respect and were not afraid to use the law to make the point. On one occasion, two individuals were charged for 'misusing the alderman in words', each fined three shillings and four pence for their cheek.

With a religious guild running the town, and compulsory church attendance, the influence of the Church was felt in every part of life. It was prominent in people's upbringing, in their thinking and in the organisation of their daily lives.

Many who were able to do so, paid the Church for indulgences as punishment for their sins. The fear of hell and having to endure a lengthy spell in purgatory was very real for most of the population. Since the Church conceded that atonement for sins could be purchased instead of remedied with good deeds, many chose to buy indulgences. This was in the belief that they were securing a shorter time in purgatory and a speedier passage to heaven. The money received by the Church was then contributed to worthy causes.

Bishop Alcock's Episcopal Register of 1489 records the payment of indulgence money to John Rutland of Parson Drove, whose house and goods had been destroyed by fire. There were many other such charitable donations made every year to local people from indulgences. They must have created a lot of paperwork and even in those days smart people were inventing ways to do such jobs more efficiently.

A number of ready-to-use indulgence forms have been discovered, dating back to around 1510. These handy forms had blank spaces to be filled in with the name of the sinner and the outcome of the indulgence.

Among the other documents to have survived from these times are many Wills. They are often very interesting in that they show the simplicity of people's material possessions, compared with how we live now. They also confirm the strong religious influence of the times.

In his Will of the fourth of August 1525, William Thornbrough, Master of the Chapel of St Mary in the Marsh, in Newton in the Isle, requested that he be 'buried before the window in which the image of the Blessed Virgin Mary looks down'. He left the chapel his land in Tydd and Newton, as well as the items he had contributed for the chapel's kitchen, brew house and dairy, a cart 'with all the gear belonging' and a candlestick.

The widow Elizabeth Fisher of Tydd St Giles, in her Will of October the fourteenth 1524, revealed even more about the items she valued. Having listed a number of gifts for the High Altar and other goods for the parish church, she proceeded to give 'Maud Brown my best gown, best kirtyll (under tunic), best gyrdyll (long hanging belt) and best cappe.' Elizabeth Fisher obviously dressed well and enjoyed a good standard of living, but left items in her Will which we wouldn't even think of mentioning now.

Moris Byrde of Wisbech, the same well placed individual who in his Will of 1525 contributed to the church tower fund, also donated eight pence for candles to light the High Altar and other altars of St Peter's Church. He left his house to his wife with the proviso that it was passed to their son on her death. To his daughter Joan he left thirty shillings as well as a bullock, a pot, a pan, a mattress and a pair of sheets. To each of his godchildren he left a sheep. He then added that all his 'household stuff' should go to his wife and that his boat should be sold.

The Church's influence could be seen even in remote places where there was neither a parish church nor a monastery. It wasn't unusual for hermits, men who had withdrawn from society for a life of religious seclusion, to serve the community in a practical way. They were known to live in isolated places where they would take care of roads, hospitals or bridges. A hermit from the Chapel of St Christopher in Outwell, for instance, looked after the bridge there for many years. Similarly, in 1457 a hermit by the name of Thomas Passhelawe was stationed at Brandon Ferry in Norfolk. By maintaining these essential, yet fairly quiet places, a hermit could serve the community while living for most of the time in the isolation he craved.

Churches were far more richly decorated at that time, their walls covered with murals depicting Biblical scenes and images of saints. Most churches had more than one altar, all of them lit by wax candles. For poor folk, whose income would never stretch to such expensive lighting, the effect of candlelight on statues, stone and images full of colour must have seemed quite magical.

In practically every church, a rood screen separated the chancel from the congregation and general public in the nave. This ornate partition of wooden or stone tracery was considered necessary because the nave, the main body of the church, was used for all sorts of town business. This would have made the church fairly noisy at times and it was important to keep the chancel private for its religious service. Above the rood screen hung a large crucifix called the High Rood, on either side of which it was usual to have statues of the Virgin Mary and St John the Apostle.

The 'new' north-west tower of St Peter's Church

Quite apart from the Church's authority, there was a rigorous legal system. Court records surviving from the early sixteenth century show the sort of penalties that were handed out for misdeeds, but they also give an interesting insight into everyday rural life.

The Court Rolls of Ramsey, Hepmangrove and Bury from 1268 to 1600 have been helpfully interpreted for modern readers. Records from court sittings of the 1530s, when the Church still controlled so much of daily life, are among the most fascinating. The calendar was still structured around saints' days and festivals, dates which would once have been as familiar to us as the names of months are now.

The record from the 'Friday before the feast of St Michael the Archangel, in the twenty-second year of the reign of King Henry VIII (1530) and the twenty-fourth year of the Lord Abbot John Wardebois' lists the cases heard by the jurors that day.

Among them was an assault on Laurence Barow by William Thomas, who 'drew blood'. William was fined three shillings and four pence.

Next up was Robert Marshall, who sounds like the local trouble maker and bad boy. He was accused of trespassing with his draught animals on his neighbour's crops, stealing his neighbours' hay and the fish from their nets. He was ordered to leave the vill of Ramsey before the Feast of St Ethelreda (June 23rd). If he dared to return within seven years he risked a fine of forty shillings.

There followed a few rulings on when and where people could graze their animals. There was an ordinance, for example, that no one should allow their pigs to wander in the lord abbot's woods for the period covering three weeks before and two weeks after the Nativity of St John the Baptist (June 24th). A fine of six shillings and eight pence was payable for any failure to comply.

In a similar ruling, no draught animals except for 'milch kine' (dairy cattle) were to be allowed on Ramsey Field from the feast of St Peter in Chains (August 1st) until the end of autumn. Breaking this rule carried a fine of three shillings and four pence.

The next item carried a reminder of the importance of maintaining local drainage ditches. All inhabitants, it was ruled, should dig and repair the ditches they were responsible for, especially those in the High Street and Little Whyte. Anything blocking the channels had to be removed before the feast of St Ethelreda and the penalty for any form of neglect of these ditches was ten shillings.

After a few more rulings of this kind, attention passed to a few troublesome women. Katherine Ellysworth was described as a 'common scold' and was ordered to restrain herself on pain of forty shillings.

The wife of William Wyse was accused of similarly annoying behaviour, with the threat of an equal fine, but for the wife of Robert Thomson things were a lot more serious. Such was her nagging that she was ordered to leave the vill before Christmas, with the usual forty shilling penalty if she failed to remove herself on time.

As the case involving bad boy Robert Marshall indicates, a great many Fenmen made their living as fishermen and watermen. The Church forbade the eating of meat on Fridays and other holy days, which kept the demand for fish high. Constant supplies were needed for the abbey kitchens of Crowland, Thorney, Ramsey, Ely and Peterborough.

Fortunately, there was an abundance of eels and fish throughout the season, food which could be preserved for the winter months. During the troubled years to come, the abbot of Crowland is said to have sent Thomas Cromwell, Henry VIII's vicar general, a barrel of pickled fish as a gift. Unfortunately, as things turned out, it didn't do the abbot much good, but more about that later.

Though life could be tough, there was at least some respite for the people of Wisbech. In a charter of 1537, the king granted permission for an annual fair to be held in King's Lynn, starting on St Valentine's Day and continuing for six days. He never did the same for Wisbech, but each year when the St Valentine fair ended and the peddlers, players and acrobats made their way from Lynn to the next fair in Stamford, they broke their journey in Wisbech. While there, they set up their stalls for a few days, selling wares and earning a little from entertaining the folk of Wisbech. In this way, the Wisbech Mart, though never established by charter, came into being. It has been held ever since, always immediately after the King's Lynn Mart in February.

Opinion was divided about the visiting entertainers. For some, they brought excitement. Music from dulcimers, trumpets, drums and cymbals filled the streets, bringing merriment and a distraction from the cold. The entertainers provided colour, diversion and laughter and even the trinkets on sale differed from the sort of merchandise usually available.

Other people were less than impressed, however. They complained strongly about the din from too many musical instruments blasting away at once.

These days, the fair still attracts complaints, but they mainly concern the wagons and lorries bunging up the car parks. Some things never really change.

Whereas other things change completely. In fact, some changes are so profound that life is altered completely and forever.

Something was going on in the central halls of power which would bring devastating consequences for many. It would lead to decades of tumult and enforced new ways of thinking for every English man and woman.

In 1534 parliament passed the Act of Supremacy. This declared that King Henry VIII was now the Supreme Head of the English Church. At that time of course, the English were Catholics and as such it was unthinkable that anyone but the Pope could lead the Church.

But whatever a person's private opinion, they had to toe the line. Any churchman who refused to accept this new state of affairs faced execution. There really was little point in argument.

Once the break with Rome was complete, the king was free to divorce Queen Catherine, his Spanish wife of twenty years, and to marry Anne Boleyn. His need for a male heir had been the driving force behind the split with Rome, but it also gave the king the freedom to reform his Church. All 'papist' influence had to go, and so the Reformation of the English Church began.

Thomas Cromwell, Henry's chief minister and vicar general, was determined to stamp out any dissension and opposition to the king's status as head of the Church. Cromwell's attention was soon focused on the monasteries.

At first, his intention was to correct the often poor and slovenly conduct within some of these religious communities, but greed soon played its part. As Cromwell's analysis of the monastic houses began, three hundred and seventy-six of the smaller ones, all with incomes below two hundred pounds a year, were deemed inefficient and closed down. Their land and other wealth were seized by the crown. The royal coffers did very well out of this, but it only whetted King Henry's appetite for more.

Thomas Cromwell's commissioners were sent all over the country to visit the remaining religious communities and to report any corruption or lax behaviour they encountered. In many cases they found nothing out of order, but ultimately it made no difference. By 1540 even the greater monasteries had been closed down and their assets seized by the king.

Carried out in the name of Reform, countless abbey buildings, shrines, even priceless manuscripts and books, were torn down or burned. The reformers removed anything they saw as idolatrous. This included the statues of saints which were part of every monastic community. They were said to encourage the worship of idols and so had to be destroyed.

The monasteries had been home to around twelve thousand monks, nuns and friars, and had provided work for thousands of servants. The more fortunate brethren were pensioned off, but any resistance was punished by execution.

Monastic property, having passed into the ownership of the king, was sold off by the Court of Augmentations, the official body tasked with selling property taken from the Church. Augmentations sold abbey buildings to local landowners wherever they could. In some of these cases, for example at Anglesey Priory in Cambridgeshire, the buildings were converted, rather than destroyed.

In some areas, the abbey churches were allowed to remain and serve the local community. Sometimes the ruins of once beautiful medieval buildings were left clinging to them, as at Crowland Abbey. A ruined arch and a few broken columns are still attached to the church, sad reminders of the monastery which once overlooked the town.

With their abbey valued at £1,217.5s.11d per annum, the Benedictine abbot and his twenty-seven monks had bowed to the inevitable. The abbot had subscribed to the Royal Supremacy in 1534 and five years later the abbey had been surrendered to the king.

It was the fate of Ely Abbey, however, which most affected the people of Wisbech and the Isle of Ely.

When Ely Abbey was dissolved on the eighteenth of November 1539, six hundred years of monastic life, dedication and care for the community came abruptly to an end. The shrine to St Ethelreda, the abbey's founder, had attracted the faithful for centuries. Among the abbey's records is a note written in 1388 which suggests that King Richard II once paid a visit to the shrine.

The monks had done what they could to smarten up the abbey for their special visitor. 'Because of the coming of the king', it was noted at the time, a dung heap had had to be removed from the door to the hostelry. Sounds like they really made an effort!

Just before the abbey's dissolution, Bishop Goodrich made a note of the fact that there were thirty-three monks under his care, ten of whom were novices. There was also an infirmary which was forced to close, its patients obliged to leave and fend for themselves.

Of far more importance to the vicar general and the king, though, was the fact that Ely Abbey was worth £1,301.8s.6d per annum.

When the authorities moved in to begin their destruction, Ely fared a little better than other monasteries. Because the abbey church was also a cathedral, it was allowed to remain. Although redundant and empty, some other buildings, such as the infirmary and the prior's chapel, also survived.

As part of Henry VIII's Reformed Church of England, Ely Cathedral began a new phase of life, but had to undergo a few changes first. Its statues, including that of the Virgin

Mary in the Lady Chapel, were either destroyed or defaced. The brightly coloured images of saints and biblical scenes which decorated the plastered walls of the nave were scraped away and whitewashed over. Even the ancient shrine to St Ethelreda was dismantled and destroyed.

Of the abbey's thirty-three monks, ten were appointed to run the king's New College in Ely when it opened in 1541. A few other brethren remained to form the Dean and Chapter of the cathedral, but the others had to leave with their small pensions and find a life elsewhere. There was no financial compensation, however, for the monastic servants who faced the almost impossible task of finding new work.

Few religious communities fared as well as Ely.

The Benedictine abbey in Thorney was valued at around £500 a year. Of the abbey buildings themselves, the reformers left little behind but ruins. Its lands, however, were considered to be of greater value and were sold by the Court of Augmentations to the Earl of Bedford. The 6,410 acres of land he acquired was chiefly comprised of valuable upland and woodland.

Very little was left standing of the Benedictine abbey in Ramsey. A lot of the stone from its demolished buildings was sent to Cambridge on Fen lighters, where it was used in the building of colleges. Extensive repairs to King's College in 1562, as well as work on Gonville and Caius College in the 1560s, made good use of the stone. Today, only the Lady Chapel and part of the once imposing gatehouse of Ramsey Abbey remain and are cared for by the National Trust.

Ramsey Abbey, which at the time of its dissolution was valued at £983.15s.3½d per annum, was granted to Sir

Richard Cromwell. He was the nephew of the mighty Thomas Cromwell and an ancestor of another mover and shaker yet to come; Oliver Cromwell.

Little remains now of Ramsey Abbey's gatehouse (with permission of the National Trust)

There had always been a strong monastic presence in King's Lynn and the monks there had run a hospital. At dissolution, of course, the hospital had to close. A local gentleman by the name of John Eyer purchased many of the town's ecclesiastical buildings, including those of the Augustinian Priory, a Dominican Friary, the White Friars' House and the Franciscan (Grey Friars') Priory. Though the great majority of these buildings were destroyed, Greyfriars' Tower was allowed to remain and serve as a landmark for ships entering the Wash. It is still there today.

The Franciscan nuns of Denny Abbey had to give up their old way of life, as did the Augustinian canons of Anglesey Priory. Though most of Anglesey's buildings were demolished, part of the old quadrangle, including the refectory, remained. These buildings were later incorporated into the house known today as the National Trust's Anglesey Abbey.

As more and more property seized from the monasteries was sold off, new, secular landowners gradually replaced ecclesiastical ones.

In the Fens, many of these new landowners were incomers, people who had little understanding of the environment they were now responsible for. As landlords, they were often harsher than the Church had been. Even more worryingly, they neglected the dykes and drains (also known as sewers) on their land which for centuries had been maintained by the monasteries. The fact that these essential flood defences were being left to decay would become a major factor in seventeenth century drainage schemes.

Meanwhile, the king was still busy with his Reforms. One of his more enduring mandates was for every parish church to have a Bible in the English language. For hundreds of years, Bibles had been written in Latin, the language of the Catholic Church. Much of the meaning of Sunday morning services had therefore been lost on ordinary people and the king wanted his subjects to be able to read the Bible for themselves.

In 1541 Bishop Goodrich of Ely was ordered to remind his parishes of their duty to acquire a Bible in English. To make this more affordable, English Bible sellers were restricted in the amount they could charge. They were not permitted to ask any more than ten shillings for an unbound Bible, though up to twelve shillings could be charged for a bound, trimmed and hasped version. Naturally, there were penalties for anyone who ignored this instruction.

Royal commands came thick and fast that year and were duly recorded in the bishop's register. On the twenty-first of October he was ordered to organise an enquiry into any images, relics or ornaments that remained in parish churches against the king's injunctions. It is likely that the statue of Our Lady, which used to stand beneath a canopy in St Peter and St Paul's in Wisbech, was removed at this time. Her empty canopy is still there today.

Something else which came to an end through Henry's Reforms was all reference to purgatory. The belief in purgatory was considered far too papist for the modern Church and so the old practice of paying for indulgences ended. Sadly, so did the charity that went with them.

Though not everyone would have missed constant reminders of purgatory, many mourned the loss of other traditions banned by King Henry. Among these were plough lights. In East Anglia, each January after Epiphany the young men of the village used to drag a plough from door to door, collecting money for candles. These lights were then put on the plough in church to bring blessings for the spring ploughing. It had been an innocent, even comforting tradition, but it was to be no more.

The clergy were told what they were allowed to preach and when. It had also been compulsory since 1535 for the royal brief, which acknowledged the king's supremacy, to be read out in church every Sunday and on feast days.

During all of this change and confusion there is little mention of the Guild of the Holy Trinity. With so much going on, it is likely that they kept their heads down. The minutes of their meetings which survive from this time show a carefully worded deference to the new regime. Each meeting's minutes now began with 'Henry VIII by the grace of God.... Defender of the Faith....and on earth the supreme head of the English Church.'

The guild, however, was left alone. For now.

One useful system introduced at this time, and which remains just as important today, was the recording of all baptisms, marriages and burials that took place in the parish. In 1538 Thomas Cromwell made the registration of these family events a legal requirement.

The registers had to be kept securely to prevent any alteration or theft. Each church was required to keep its registers in a chest secured with two locks. The parish chest, thought to be the original, can still be seen in St Peter's Church.

As a further deterrent against fraud, a copy of the registers had to be sent each year to the bishop. Cromwell's need for so much security was based on the prevention of false inheritance claims. The legal system was having to waste far too much time on claims to family fortunes supported by falsified statements of age and rights. Registration was perhaps one of the vicar general's better moves.

16th century chest in St Peter's Church (with permission of the parish church)

Far more basic concerns meanwhile were troubling the men of Wisbech. On the twenty-first of July 1539, twenty-one cobblers assembled at Mill Hill (at the eastern end of modern day Hill Street) to demand an increase in pay. The fifteen pence they were receiving for a 'dosyn shoos sewyng' was not enough, they said. They wanted a rise to eighteen pence. Though it's uncertain how long it would have taken them to sew a dozen shoes, at a time when a loaf of bread cost a penny, fifteen pence would not have gone far. Sadly, their protest didn't achieve much. A few of them were apprehended, but most of the cobblers fled and the matter was dropped. The bishop, who was asked to decide on the matter, concluded that their protest had been more about promoting the shoemakers' interests than opposing the law.

Although the bishop used common sense in dealing with this situation, the legal system was generally harsh. Some laws seem ridiculous today and one in particular reflects the increasing prejudice and fear concerning witchcraft. An Act of 1541prohibited the use of enchantment and sorcery to find treasure and obtain stolen goods.

At around this time, a man by the name of John Partriche of Holbeach was suspected of using sorcery to steal goods from his parish church. Despite his protests of innocence, his so-called friends turned against him and ransacked his house. John was so confident of his blamelessness that he appealed to the Court of the Star Chamber. During his hearing he alleged that others in the town were using the art of necromancy and that he was, to use a modern term, being set up. Annoyingly, records aren't clear about the outcome of his case, but it shows how quickly opinion could turn against someone as soon as there was a whiff of witchcraft in the air.

As a brief explanation, the Court of the Star Chamber took its name from the ceiling decoration of the room at

Westminster in which the court sat. The court consisted of privy councillors and judges and was known for its resistance to the corruption which could affect other courts. Unlike them, it was not bound by common law and didn't depend on a jury. Prominent people, who had always been able to use their influence to avoid punishment for their crimes, stood no chance against the Star Chamber. It was eventually abolished in 1641 by Charles I.

While on the subject of the law, it seems a good time to mention parliament. Parliament had first come into being in 1275 when Edward I had summoned representatives from every shire and town in England to discuss the raising of taxes. It wasn't until 1523, though, that the right to free speech was introduced by Sir Thomas More. King Henry VIII increased parliament's powers in 1547 and allowed members to meet in St Stephen's Chapel in the Palace of Westminster. The House of Lords was the upper house, the Commons the lower, as is still the case today.

The aging king was nearing the end of his days by this time and had plenty to look back on. Among his various deeds, he had freed his country from papal control, dissolved the monasteries and enhanced the status of parliament.

Though his initial aim had been Reform, he would be remembered more as the tyrant who had made thousands of monks and monastery servants redundant and had abandoned the sick and disabled to be thrown out of closing hospitals. He had effectively removed the old social services system and had done nothing to replace it.

He had at least allowed the ancient hospital of St Bartholomew to continue, granting it to the City of London in 1546 and endowing it with property, but such actions were rare. The king had been more effective in founding new schools. The New College was established in Ely in 1541 and in the same year the Schola Regia, or King's School, was founded in the precincts of Peterborough Cathedral. It aimed to 'train in piety' and educate the cathedral choristers and other Peterborough boys. Though the school has long since moved to new premises, its close relationship with the cathedral continues.

It is hard to imagine great sorrow on the old king's passing in 1547. Perhaps the Fenlanders hoped for an easier time under Henry's young son, Edward. If so, they were about to be disappointed.

CHAPTER THREE

Chop and Change; The Times of Edward VI and Mary I

Although Edward VI was only nine years old in 1547 when he came to the throne and ruled with the aid of a regency council, he wasted no time in continuing his father's work.

The Reformed English Church which Edward inherited from Henry VIII was still essentially Catholic and he was determined to free it from its old influences. Under him, the Church of England would become Protestant and for the first time its clergy would be permitted to marry.

First of all, he set about shutting down Church run colleges, chantries and any hospitals which had escaped the last purge. As before, their land and other assets were seized by the crown and anything without a resale value was destroyed.

There were a number of chantries in Wisbech (chapels endowed for the singing of masses for the departed) which had been part of the community for centuries. One of these was St Martin's on the north bank of the Nene, one which had acquired considerable wealth over the years.

Closing down the small chapel wouldn't have taken long. Its assets were seized and were soon swelling the royal coffers. The chantry land and buildings were duly let to a Mr Johnston on a forty year lease. However, perhaps due to the pressure of work caused by the acquisition of so much wealth, the authorities seem to have slipped up. Somehow, the collection of rent was allowed to lapse and it wasn't until more than a century later, in 1670, that an eagle-eyed book keeper noticed the problem. He sent a bill to the town bailiff. The arrears amounted to thirty pounds plus a fee of five pounds; a considerable amount for the times.

Eager to press on with his Reforms, the king sent commissioners to all parts of the country. They were tasked with surveying the land holdings of each town, together with its guilds, schools and remaining religious buildings.

They looked carefully at vulnerable areas such as the Fens, where flooding had always been a problem, assessing the maintenance that was being carried out on sea and river defences.

It was not long before the commissioners arrived in Wisbech.

Their attention was soon focused on the town's leading religious guild. Two commissioners met churchwardens and the alderman of the Guild of the Holy Trinity in Ely to begin a detailed assessment of the guild's wealth and its role in the community. They took into account its grammar school, charitable deeds and its work as landlord in repairing river banks and sea walls. The commissioners acknowledged in their report that such repairs were essential and had to continue against the 'rages of the sea.'

Quite separately, they recommended that some chapels which served outlying communities should be allowed to remain. One of these was the Chapel of Corpus Christi at Fendyke, four miles from Wisbech.

Despite what appears to have been a reasonably polite meeting, there could have been no doubt that the guild's days were numbered.

The Guild of the Holy Trinity, which had operated in Wisbech for more than a hundred and fifty years, held its last meeting on the twenty-fourth of June 1547. It must have been a very sombre occasion.

Page from a minute book dated 1379 of the Guild of the Holy Trinity (with permission of Wisbech and Fenland Museum)

The guild had become very wealthy, as shown by the list of assets in its final accounts. Among the property listed was land in the Timber Market, a messuage (a house with outbuildings) by the castle dyke, a quarter of an acre in Old Field, two acres in East Field, five in Harecroft, four on 'castle land' and two in Sandyland. In all, the guild owned two hundred and seventy-seven acres and three roods of land, the guild hall, an almshouse near St Peter's churchyard and other messuages.

Even during these uncertain times, there was no pause in the need for drainage work. Decayed dykes, neglected river banks and the unstoppable process of nature herself, all contributed to the workload.

In 1547 the Commission of Sewers held an urgent meeting in Upwell. The commissioners, Geoffrey Colvile, Edmund Beaupre and Richard Everard, met to assess the destruction caused by the recent flooding of eight thousand acres in Upwell, Outwell and Marshland. Three hundred homes had been damaged or completely destroyed.

They concluded that the disaster had been caused by the poor condition of the river and sewers (drains) in and around March and which ran through Wisbech. The waterways and drains had failed to cope with recent high rainfall and the volume of water coming downstream from inland counties.

The commissioners ordered immediate work to be done on the decayed sewers and a new sluice gate of stone or timber to be built at Upwell. There was, as is usual for the times, no mention of any relief for the newly homeless. They would have had to fend for themselves, but at least the area would be safe from flooding for a while.

Meanwhile the king, having done away with the town's old order, was about to introduce a new one.

In 1549 King Edward VI granted Wisbech a charter which elevated the town to a corporate borough. Wisbech was declared to be one body incorporated as the 'inhabitants of the town of Wisbech within the Isle of Ely in the county of Cambridge.' The new borough, also referred to as a corporation, included Leverington, Newton in the Isle, Tydd, Elm, Emneth, West Walton and Walpole. It was granted a common seal for the transaction of its affairs.

The charter, of course, came at a cost. King Edward's commissioners had made a thorough assessment of the old guild's possessions and land, together with its annual rental income. Deductions had been made from this sum to allow for the guild's charitable payments, as well as the salaries of the school master and other personnel.

These calculations resulted in a fee of £260.10s.10d payable to the king. In return, Wisbech received its charter and new status as a corporate borough. Land and messuages which had once belonged to the guild and had been taken by the king were now graciously granted back to the town.

Bishop Goodrich of Ely, who was clearly in good odour with the young monarch, took an active part in smoothing the path for Wisbech. He managed to secure the return of some of the guild's valuables which were then sold for the benefit of the borough.

Among the corporation's earliest minutes is a record of the sale by the church wardens and parishioners of some of the guild's treasure. The items sold included a silver gilt cross, a chalice and a pair of silver saucers. They were purchased by two London goldsmiths for £44.16s. This money went a long way in Wisbech. It provided uniforms for the local militia, a sluice of brick and timber at the 'little Eau' near Tydd, plus essential repairs of the church and market cross. It also paid for rag stone paving for the market place and repairs to the sea banks. The new borough was clearly making a positive start.

The charter was very specific about how the corporation was to be run. It stated that on the first day of November each year the town's householders should gather in the common hall (or town hall) in Ship Lane to elect 'ten men' for the coming year. The common hall is thought to have been the old guild hall building, but unfortunately nothing remains to tell us for sure.

Once elected for the year, the ten men were responsible for the administration of corporation land for the common good of the borough. Among their other duties was the distribution of three pounds and fifteen shillings a year to the poor, so in many ways they were taking over the roles of the old guild.

Some tasks, however, remained in the same experienced hands as before. Local drainage continued to be the responsibility of the Commission of Sewers.

King Edward's charter also provided for a grammar school. One already existed, of course, the guild having founded a grammar school in 1379, so it was really a case of granting it new authority.

The ten men were tasked with the appointment of a new school master who had to be educated in Latin and Greek and to be of good moral standing. Master Henry Ogle was duly appointed and paid an annual salary of twelve pounds. The Bishop of Ely kept his old role at the school with overall rights of 'visitation, reformation and correction'. As part of this duty, the bishop paid the school a visit every four years. On these occasions the senior boy had to deliver a Latin oration in his lordship's presence. The poor lad's knees must have been knocking!

At around this time, land was granted for the building of a new school house in Ship Lane. The school must have outgrown its single small room over the church porch and its move to new premises next to the common hall in Ship Lane gave the school room to grow.

Meanwhile, the young king was still working on his Reforms. In 1550 he ordered that all church altars should be removed and destroyed before Christmas Day. All over the country, altars were replaced with simple communion tables, usually placed in the nave rather than the chancel, as before. At around the same time, the vestments worn by the clergy were simplified, plain surplices replacing traditional, elaborate vestments.

It can only be imagined what the parishioners of St Peter and St Paul's in Wisbech thought to all this. Many Wisbech men were craftsmen who worked with wood and stone, people who would have appreciated beautifully made objects. It is hard to believe that they were indifferent to the removal of so many familiar treasures, especially when it came to the tearing out of the rood screen.

For as long as anyone could remember, there had been a rood screen, most likely of ornately carved wood, separating the chancel and nave of St Peter's. It was a sturdy structure, capable of supporting the musicians who had always sat on top of the screen to play. Parts of the liturgy had also been sung from there. But, despite its beauty and usefulness, it was seen now as no more than a papist symbol and had to be destroyed.

King Edward had brought a huge amount of change to his kingdom, but his time was running out. His reign came to an abrupt end after only six years, the boy succumbing to sickness and early death.

The people of Wisbech, having witnessed the transition of their town into a corporate borough in a Protestant land, must have hoped for a few uneventful years in which to get used to the new order.

That wasn't quite what happened, though.

Mary

In 1553 Edward's sister Mary inherited the throne. She was a Catholic.

Practically the first thing Queen Mary did was to reunite her country with the Pope in Rome and restore the old faith. Cardinal Pole, the new Archbishop of Canterbury, worked hard to reinstate England's Catholic foundations.

It was too late to save the monasteries; the heaps of rubble which were all that remained of most of them were beyond resurrection, but church services were more easily returned to their old format. The Latin Mass was brought back, as were altars and any statues and images which had not been smashed to pieces. Some churches even had their rood screens restored, but in most cases, as in Wisbech, their destruction had been too complete for any hope of that.

Once more under Roman Catholic control, priests were no longer allowed to marry. Any married Protestant clergy and priests unwilling to revert to Catholicism escaped abroad if they had any sense. In 1555 parliament passed a series of heresy laws which made it illegal to remain a Protestant. Anyone who refused to comply faced death.

Again, the English were expected to toe the line and accept without question a ruthless barrage of change. The simpler church services in English, which they were probably getting used to, were done away with in favour of the Latin Mass. It was safer for the sake of a quiet life just to go along with it. Anyone brave or silly enough to voice an objection was presumably silenced by what happened next.

Word may have reached the Fen people in October 1555 about the fate of the old Archbishop of Canterbury and other prominent Protestants. Thomas Cranmer, Archbishop and author of the Book of Common Prayer, Nicholas Ridley, the Bishop of London, and Hugh Latimer, the Bishop of Worcester, all of whom had refused to recant their Protestant beliefs, were publicly burned at the stake in Oxford.

But such horrors were not just happening out of sight and out of mind from Wisbech. They were happening locally too.

And figureheads such as Cranmer, Latimer and Ridley weren't the only people being put to death for their refusal to re-embrace Catholicism. It was also happening to ordinary folk.

William Wolsey was the constable of Outwell, Upwell and Welney. Though he attended church, his refusal to take part in the Mass was spotted by a local Justice of the Peace. Wolsey was duly dismissed from his position of authority, arrested and summoned to the Ely Assizes.

Dr Fuller, the Bishop of Ely's chancellor, and John Christopherson, the Dean of Norwich, tried to make Wolsey see sense. They demanded that he 'meddle no further with the scriptures as it did become a layman as he was, to do.' Dr Fuller lent Wolsey a book written by the Catholic Bishop of Lincoln, hoping that it would change his mind. The book had the opposite effect, however, and was returned to Dr Fuller with Wolsey's comments scribbled all over it. Dr Fuller, whose favourite book had been defaced and who was getting nowhere, sent Wolsey to be dealt with by the Wisbech Assizes. Wolsey was duly imprisoned in the castle.

Joining him in prison was Robert Pygot, a Wisbech builder and painter and the tenant of the old chantry of St Martin's on the north bank of the river. He had been arrested for refusing to attend church on Sundays and had been dispatched to prison by the judge of Assizes, Sir Clement Hygham.

The damp and miserable conditions of Wisbech Castle did nothing to weaken the convictions of either man, despite the further attempts of Dr Fuller to persuade them to give up their Protestant ideals and save their lives.

Wolsey and Pygot, later known as the Wisbech Martyrs, were transferred to Ely gaol. On the sixteenth of October 1555 they were taken to the city's Cathedral Green where they were bound with chains, fastened to a stake and burned.

Whether or not by coincidence, this turned out to be the same day as Latimer and Ridley were put to death in Oxford.

While still in captivity at Wisbech Castle, William Wolsey had written to a fellow Protestant, a smith of Upwell called Richard Denton. In his letter, Wolsey had tried to persuade Denton to be true to his heart and speak openly about his beliefs. Understandably, the smith wasn't over keen on the idea of martyrdom and kept quiet. Shortly after Wolsey's horrifying death, Denton is said to have commented that his friend had been right and that he, Denton, ought to be braver and more honest about his beliefs. He had, however, no wish to be burned.

Not long after this admission, his house was mysteriously set on fire. In an attempt to rescue his belongings, Denton and two others died in the flames. Perhaps his neighbours thought he should share his old friend's punishment?

The fate of Wolsey and Pygot was recorded in John Foxe's Book of Martyrs, which was published in 1563 when Protestants were once again free to worship. A copy of the book was placed in every cathedral and collegiate church.

In 1635 a Wisbech gentleman by the name of Robert Goodridge left three volumes of John Foxe's work to St Peter and St Paul's Church. A wooden memorial plaque was carved to commemorate this gift and was hung above a desk supporting the three volumes. The plaque still hangs in the church today and a copy of John Foxe's book is held in the library of Wisbech and Fenland Museum.

Print from Foxe's Book of Martyrs showing the death of Wolsey and Pigot (with permission of Wisbech and Fenland Museum)

Mary's reign wasn't just dangerous for Protestants. Anyone whose views or interests made them stand out from the crowd could find themselves in trouble. In such a culture of fear, it is hardly surprising that anything related to witchcraft aroused suspicion.

The Londoner John Dee was a mathematician, astronomer and astrologer who was fascinated by the occult. In 1553, Dee's research and experiments led to his being accused of attempting to kill Queen Mary by sorcery. He was imprisoned at Hampton Court. After a few frightening months he was released, but it was a stern warning. Any suspicion of witchcraft was a very dangerous thing.

Queen Mary's reign lasted a mere five years, but would not easily be forgotten. By the time of her death in 1558, she had put nearly three hundred Protestants to death by burning, for which she had earned the title 'Bloody Mary'. However, her illness and consequently short reign had given her insufficient time to complete England's reversion to Catholicism.

And anyway, all she had done would be swept away when her younger sister succeeded her.

CHAPTER FOUR

Prison, Plague and Gewgaws; The Times of Elizabeth I

For the third time in eleven years, the English people were drinking to the health of a new monarch. More than a few of them must have had misgivings, especially considering all the ups and downs of the last three reigns.

The young Queen Elizabeth, perhaps aware of these concerns, trod a little more gently than her predecessors. Like her brother Edward VI, she was a reformist, but understood that forcing the country into yet another religious U-turn would earn her little popularity.

However, Elizabeth did not delay in bringing in her own brand of Reforms. In 1559, once the country's allegiance to the Pope had again been broken, the Act of Uniformity was passed. This set out how the new queen's Church would be run.

In many ways the Church returned to how it had been during the time of Edward VI; a Reformed Church which held on to a few symbols of Roman Catholicism. Some features, such as priests' vestments, were kept from Queen Mary's rule, but many more items were deemed too papist and were removed. Any restored rood screens, altars, wall paintings and statues were hastily done away with. Again.

In the background, and chipping away at the establishment with their views, was a group of non-conformist Protestants called Puritans. They wanted Church practices to be simplified even further and, although Elizabeth rejected many of their ideas, she agreed to a few of them.

The word 'priest', for instance, was considered unsuitable for the new regime and so clergymen became known as ministers.

The Latin Mass was once again replaced by a simpler service in English and fewer prayers were learned by rote. People were encouraged to use their own words and to make their prayers more personal.

Some of the old ecclesiastical land and property which had been restored to the Church by Mary was once again annexed by the crown. This can't have gone down well with the clergy, but most of them had more pressing concerns. Catholic priests faced a choice between converting to Protestantism and leaving the country. Meanwhile, Anglican ministers who had gone into exile during Mary's reign, returned to take the places of emigrating Catholics.

Queen Elizabeth toned down her title a little, becoming Supreme Governor of the English Church, rather than its Supreme Head, as her father and brother had styled themselves. She brought back the Book of Common Prayer introduced in the time of Edward VI and imposed a fine of twelve pence for non-attendance at church on Sundays.

Catholics were not persecuted, but life would certainly become harder for them later.

So, yet again there were new rules for the Fen people to get used to. All they had to do was to keep their heads down, go to church on Sundays and keep any objections to themselves.

But in other respects they did not always behave well. The good folk of Wisbech seem to have fallen out with their neighbours on a regular basis. By the early 1560s problems were brewing between them and the people of March and Doddington over the joint use of Norwood Common, located between March and Wisbech.

Bishop Cox of Ely had already given the people of March and Doddington a sound telling-off in his letter of 1560 in which he accused them of lawlessness and stealing their neighbours' cattle.

'...I understand ye fall to your olde practise...and pynne your neighbours cattle...Saye not but ye have had warnynge.'

Their behaviour had clearly not improved a year later, when the bishop had to write to them again. Inhabitants of the Wisbech Hundred were complaining that March folk were denying them proper joint usage of the common and that their cattle were still being stolen. The bishop charged the people of March in the queen's name to allow Wisbech folk peaceful access to the common and to refrain from nicking their livestock.

The traditional rivalry between Wisbech and March lives on in the occasional Saturday night fracas between lads of the two towns.

Wisbech was not always the innocent party. Later that same year, its inhabitants managed to get themselves involved in another dispute concerning a different piece of common land. It seems they had been trying to stop people from Sutton St Edmunds having free access to four thousand acres of drained common land which lay between the two towns.

It took a stern letter from the queen herself to sort the matter out. On the twelfth of May 1561 Queen Elizabeth wrote to the Wisbech town bailiff, John Gallant, ordering that the people of Sutton be allowed full access and undisturbed passage over the common on their way to Wisbech. This was to be until the bishop's chancellor made a final decision on the matter. The inhabitants of Wisbech were further informed that if they continued to make trouble they would incur a fine of five hundred pounds. This seems to have done the trick and in the end an agreement was reached. The land in question was later divided into two areas, Wisbech Fen and Sutton St Edmunds Common.

Apart from these hiccups, life in Wisbech seems to have been fairly peaceful. In accordance with Edward VI's charter, its ten men continued to be elected each year and kept the minutes of their meetings diligently.

It is rather mysterious therefore, that the records covering the period of Queen Mary's reign were lost. Curiously missing also were the records of baptisms, marriages and burials in the parish for the same period. Since all documents from 1558, the start of Elizabeth's reign, remained miraculously in place, it would appear that everything from Mary's time was deliberately removed. Wisbech is not the only place where this occurred. It seems there was a widespread attempt to erase all memory of Mary's reign and it certainly doesn't help our knowledge of local history.

The corporation's records give a detailed account of the elections of 1564. As had occurred each year since the time of Edward VI, on the first of November the townspeople voted for ten officers who would serve for the next twelve months. These 'honest and sober men', whose incomes had to be at least forty shillings a year, were Richard Everard, Robert Scotred, Robert Best, Edward Wilkes, Edward Storeye, Thomas Butcher, William Day, Nicholas Mychell, Alexander Coxson and Henry Markham.

The following day, these newly elected officers met in the common hall to elect a bailiff. Rather than choose one of the ten, as would become normal practice in later years, an eleventh man, Richard Best was chosen. As bailiff, he was responsible for the rent collected from borough land and tenements, but needed the full agreement of the ten men on how the town's money was allocated. He received a small payment of £1.6s.8d; presumably his other income made a larger salary unnecessary. The stipend of £13.6s.8d a year paid to Mr Rastall the schoolmaster was more like a living wage.

Humphrey Turner, who was paid by the corporation for singing and 'maintaining God's service' in the church, was paid £3.6s.8d a year. Philip Wright, who was appointed the town wayt (watch), earned a mere £1.13s.4d per annum. His duties included patrolling the streets at night and waking townsfolk on dark winter mornings by playing a musical instrument similar to a trumpet. A scavenger was also appointed, to keep the streets and market place clean. He was paid ten shillings a year for his work, as was Edward Wilkes, the clerk appointed to keep the bailiff's accounts.

The new bailiff was given a list of the corporation's leases and an inventory of items belonging to the town. Among the items listed were twenty-eight pewter platters, three spits for the kitchen chimney, a bow and a case of arrows, items of body armour and eight old windows, recently removed from the common hall.

It was then decided that the ten men, the bailiff, the vicar and the school master would meet on the first Tuesday of every month in the common hall. There they would hear and settle any neighbourhood disputes arising at the time.

It became customary for these gentlemen to dine together after each monthly meeting at one of their homes and for everyone to contribute four pence towards the cost of the meal.

However delightful these culinary incentives, attendance at the monthly meetings wasn't as good as it should have been and the rules had to be sharpened up. In 1569 it was decided that anyone absent without notice should be excluded from all further meetings and never be readmitted.

Perhaps it was the freezing weather that put them off leaving home. Although the country was still in the grip of a mini ice age and hard winters were the norm, the winters of 1570 and 1571 were so dreadful, and resulted in so much loss of life, that local people were inspired to write about them.

Thanks to the accounts that survive, we know that in 1570 the snow began to fall ten days before Christmas and continued relentlessly for many weeks. By Christmas, the snow was deeper than anyone could recall ever seeing before, yet it went on falling, bringing no respite until February.

When at last the thaw set in, it brought more problems. The huge volume of melting snow created deep and devastating floods. Most of East Anglia was covered in water, all the way from Wisbech to Yarmouth.

When the spring finally came, work began to repair all the damage. There was so much to be done that the Commission of Sewers had to sort the jobs in order of priority.

One of the most urgent was the sea bank protecting Wisbech. The section between Leverington and Core Corner in Wisbech, and from there to the Old Market, had been broken down by flood water. The commissioners ordered the landowners to the north of Wisbech to start work immediately on building the banks up to a greater height and width.

Landowners in Barton (near the junction of modern day Barton Road and North Brink) were also set to work. They had to build a raised causeway of just over a metre in height and two and a half metres in width, to be called Gigg's Drove.

Another high priority job was the construction of a new sluice at the Horseshoe in Leverington. At the same time, the silted-up stretch of river between Guyhirn and the sea had to be scoured out and widened to eighteen metres, its depth increased to three metres. All this work was achieved, of course, with simple spades and plenty of backache.

Also high on the commissioners' list was work on the sea bank between Tydd Gote and the Horseshoe and from there to Crabbe Marsh Gate. The people of Tydd, Newton and Leverington were ordered to build the bank up to six metres above the salt marsh and to do so quickly, before winter came.

Unfortunately, it wasn't done quickly at all. Work on the sea banks was still unfinished when the autumn storms of 1571 began.

In October a violent storm of wind and rain hit the east coast. The weakened and incomplete sea banks were no match for the huge waves which broke over and through them, overflowing Leverington, Newton, Wisbech and the surrounding area to a depth of several feet.

In Parson Drove, the entire chancel of St John the Baptist's Church was washed away, as were many homes.

An English chronicler, Raphael Holinshed, was one writer whose account of the storm of October 1571 has survived. His spellings of local place names have been kept in, out of interest.

'The sea broke in between Wisbech and Walsoken and at the Cross Keies, drowning Tilneie and Old Lin, Saint Marie, Teding Saint Marie, Tid Saint John, Wauple, Walton, Walsoken, Emnie, Jarmans and Stow Bridge...Wisbech, Guihorne, Parson Drove and Hobhouse...'

Holinshed went on to describe what happened to a couple living in the almshouse at Hobhouse, near Guyhirn. One night, the flood water had become so deep that the walls of the house caved in. The man and woman were awoken by the sudden blast of cold air through the broken down walls and the wind which blew away their bed cover. The man got out of bed to reach for his clothes but fell over in the water which was rapidly filling the house. Fearing that the place was about to collapse, he picked up his wife and carried her out, managing to save them both.

The writer mentioned other places that suffered damage, such as the 'garden or tennis place and a bowling allie' in Wisbech, which were surrounded by brick walls and worth twenty pounds a year to the owner. It isn't often that places of entertainment crop up in local records of that time, so it is interesting to note that both bowls and tennis were available to anyone able to afford them.

Far more serious losses were mentioned by Holinshed. Master Thimblebie, for example, lost two hundred and twenty sheep and Master Dimoke four hundred. There were many other animals killed in the floods, among them an estimated twenty thousand cattle.

Holland, Leverington, Long Sutton, Holbeach and the Chapel of St Mary in the Marsh in Newton in the Isle were all seriously flooded, as was the whole of Marshland. Holinshed added that little remained of the sea bank between West Lynn and Magdalen Bridge and that further away, in St Ives near Huntingdon, boats could be rowed over the churchyard wall without touching the top.

There are plenty of memories of extreme Fenland weather which have been passed down the generations, enhanced a bit here and there. One relates to another serious flood of 1575, when heavy February rain, followed by high spring tides, caused the river to burst its banks. Fierce gales battered the coast and the sea banks were unable to hold back the stormy sea. Huge expanses of Fenland and Marshland were flooded and sailing ships were driven inland. One of them, so the story goes, ended up on the roof of a house. The sailors apparently managed to lower themselves into an upper chamber of the house, where they rescued a woman about to give birth.

Centuries of catastrophic floods, and the loss and misery that went with them, eventually led to the invention of the windmill.

Between 1570 and 1580 George Carlton, the Governor of Wisbech Castle and local landowner, erected what appear to have been the earliest mills used for draining. His mills were installed to protect the newly embanked area around Waldersea, Coldham, Ring's End, Hobhouse, Elm Leam, Redmore Dyke and Begdale.

Mills had been used in towns and villages to grind grain since the 1100s, but had not until now been adapted for use in drainage.

They were very effective, so long as there was enough wind to turn their sails, but they were not popular with

Fenmen. The great structures, with their creaking, circling sails, visible from miles around on the wide horizon, alarmed the local people who had probably never seen windmills in the towns. The mills became known locally as 'gewgaws'. They were so disliked that Master Carlton had trouble in hiring enough labourers to build and maintain them.

And that wasn't his only problem. The old enemy, silt build-up in the river outfall to the sea, was a real obstacle. In 1579 Master Carlton applied to the Bishop of Ely and the Commission of Sewers to have the river cleansed and scoured again between Guyhirn and the sea. Until it was done, he argued, his mills would labour in vain to empty water into blocked sewers. Whether or not he received a useful response, it seems the Fens were not quite ready for his windmills. Their time would come.

Other types of Fenland control, however, were running with comparative ease.

Overseeing the fishing rights of local landowners were the fennifers. Their duties included making sure that closed seasons and other local rules were observed. The 1579 Manorial Court Rolls of Glatton listed the fines and penalties that had been issued for breaches of bylaws and regulations. Among them were cases reported by the fennifers of Whittlesey Mere.

One entry concluded that 'we ffynd yt Thomas Hansun and Rychard Bacton dyd not kepe the rawght day but dyd cast on ye Saturday contrary to....'

Another entry read 'we ffynd yt William Gardner ye yowngr is to be amersed for yt he hathe forsaken his father in his part of ffysshyng wt owt lycens....'

From these records it appears that fishing was prohibited on Saturdays, as was fishing without a licence. The fines imposed usually amounted to just a few pennies, but bearing in mind the cost of bread at a penny, a fine of three or four pence would have made a sizeable hole in a poor man's pocket.

Meanwhile back in Wisbech, the town bridge was in need of repair. There had been a bridge over the river by the Old Market since at least 1326, but its timber construction meant that it had to be repaired or rebuilt every few decades. Whenever money had had to be raised for the work, it seems there had always been disputes. In 1533, when the bridge's south-east pier had been in imminent danger of collapse, and everyone was arguing about who should stump up the necessary funds, the bishop had had to chip in. He had agreed to share the cost with the landowners to the north of the river in order to prevent any further delays, not to mention a horrible accident.

By 1583 the bridge had again reached the point where it needed to be rebuilt. The borough's ten men met on the ninth of September and decided 'that the carpenters and labourers should begin work on the great bridge of Wysbiche.' This time they were determined to do the job properly. Three of the ten men rode to St Ives near Huntingdon to look at the bridge there and learn about its construction.

Money, of course, had to be raised and in the following January it was agreed that every householder in the town should contribute. They would be in good company, though. The queen herself was due to pay a share of the cost this time; of the total £51.4s.10d needed, her majesty was expected to pay £33.8s. For some reason, however, she only managed to send £30, leaving a deficit of £3.8s. In the end, this had to be met out of town funds.

Signature of Elizabeth I on a letter to Henry IV of France (with permission of Wisbech and Fenland Museum)

At last, the project was completed. The new timber bridge was built on a substantial brick base on each side. The ten men decided that in future the cost of bridge repairs should be shared with the people of Elm, Upwell and Outwell.

The Commission of Sewers always had a full workload. In 1581, at a meeting attended by local landowners John Peyton and Thomas Hewar, it was re-established that Wisbech was responsible for maintaining the old Well Stream, as well as the sea banks, as far as the stone cross near Emneth. This cross, which marked the boundary between Elm and Wisbech, had once been known as the Spittal Cross, the site of a medieval leper hospital.

Between the cross and the Elm flood gates, responsibility for the maintenance of the river and its banks fell to Elm. However, any work on the stretch of river between Elm bridge and Friday Bridge was to be charged to her majesty. This was because that particular piece of land had once belonged to Crowland Abbey before it was annexed by the crown. It is to be hoped that the queen managed a full payment when asked.

A Little Care in the Community

The monasteries had always been responsible for the care of the poor, but their dissolution had brought care in the community to an abrupt end. There were no more alms for the starving and no more healing or shelter for the sick. The monastic system had been far from perfect, but it had certainly been better than nothing.

The poor and sick were left to beg for scraps of food, clothed in rags and without shelter. The enclosure of common land had added to the problem, ending a traditional way of life for thousands. The loss of long-held rights of access to common land, on which to graze their animals and to gather firewood, had led to widespread homelessness and starvation. (More about this in Chapter Eight.)

The mounting problems of poverty could be ignored no longer.

In 1552, during Queen Mary's reign, the number of the needy in each parish had started to be recorded, so that some kind of support could be provided. Then, in the early years of Elizabeth's reign, Justices of the Peace had been authorised to raise funds to support those in need.

A more comprehensive system was now being established in which poverty was assessed and put into one of three categories. The first category was for the deserving poor; orphaned children, the aged, sick, blind, lame and lepers. These people were deemed incapable of work and therefore had to be helped. Where possible, they were provided with food and clothing and accommodated in almshouses. Children were placed in orphanages or apprenticed to tradesmen.

The second category was for the able bodied poor. These were people who wanted to work but were unable to find employment. Apprenticeships were found for some and others were set to work in their own homes.

The third category was treated less sympathetically. These were considered to be the undeserving poor, vagrants who chose not to work and who roamed the countryside, often in gangs, stealing and generally making a nuisance of themselves. When apprehended by the constable, they were whipped and sent back to their own parishes.

In Wisbech, the duties of the ten men were extended to the provision of poor aid. In 1576, as well as being responsible for placing poor children in apprenticeships, they began to act as trustees for the property of the widows and orphans entrusted to their care. The funds were invested at eight percent to provide an income for the widows and their children until they reached maturity. The original invested sum had to be repaid to the widow at the end of the term.

The ten men were also authorised to advance small loans of up to twenty shillings to poor families to set them up in work. As well as this, sums were donated to keep parentless children in orphanages.

The officers also acted as trustees for the charitable donations and bequests given by local people for the poor. In 1583 a total of £48.18s.9d was invested.

The responsibilities of these ten busy men included the administration of fees payable for the tolling of church bells to mark the deaths of townspeople.

Other demands on the public purse stand out in sharp contrast to its poor relief. Like other towns, Wisbech was expected to contribute towards the supply of lambs and calves for the queen's table. Quite how happily these compulsory donations were made has never been mentioned.

Another responsibility of the ten men was to check the churchwardens' accounts, including sums collected for the poor. The figures were then sent to the Justice of the Peace for a final check. The corporation seems to have taken its responsibility towards the poor very seriously.

The wealthy were doing their bit too. In his Will of 1593, John Bend left a messuage later known as The Butchers' Arms Inn and sixteen acres of land in trust for the poor of Leverington and Parson Drove. This was to help them buy stock for setting up small businesses or to help them with rent. A few years later, in 1603, Margaret Bend left £50, the interest from which was to pay six shillings and eight pence a year to the poor of Parson Drove.

By 1597 it had become a legal requirement for every district to appoint an Overseer of the Poor. His job was to set the poor rate for the district based on the number of old, blind, sick and poor recorded in the parish register. This poor rate was then collected from the property owners of the parish and distributed to the needy.

The Overseer was responsible for finding work for the able bodied poor. Where no work was available locally, a kind of cottage industry was set up in homes of the impoverished. Stocks of raw materials, perhaps wool or flax for spinning, were sent to their homes. The finished goods were then sold to provide an income and keep the families in their own homes. This system kept families together and seems so much better than the workhouses which came in later times.

Plague

Fear of the plague was never far away. Outbreaks of the disease occurred sporadically and the devastation of the Black Death, which had swept through the country in the mid 1300s, had never really been forgotten.

In 1585 people living in the hamlet of Guyhirn began to fall sick. As more and more of them succumbed to the sickness, the dreaded word 'plague' began to be spoken. Money was raised in Wisbech to support the victims and the sum of £4.15s.5d was sent to Guyhirn.

Very little was understood at the time about how the disease was spread. It was believed to be carried through the air by bad smells caused by insanitary conditions. One thing that had been worked out, though, was that the spread of sickness could be controlled by reducing the movement of people and goods in and out of an affected area. No one, therefore, was permitted to enter or leave Guyhirn while the plague ran its course. Except, of course, for whoever it was from Wisbech who had taken the money to Guyhirn.

As a further precaution against infection, the streets and open drains of Wisbech were cleaned out to reduce the evil smells that emanated from the rotting waste usually dumped there.

The ten men then held a meeting to plan their strategy in the event of the plague reaching Wisbech. They decided to divide the town into wards, creating ten smaller areas which would be easier to control. The ten wards were:

Timber Ward. From the south end of St Peter's churchyard, encompassing the Timber Market and reaching as far out of town as New Common Bridge.

Church Ward. From the south-western side of the market place as far as the old castle gate (near the present day Clarkson Memorial).

Castle Ward. All the buildings to the north of Deadman's Lane (modern day Love Lane), the western side of the Timber Market to Swillingburn Field, which was beyond Tillery Field.

South Ward. All the buildings along the south bank of the river.

Barton Ward. All the buildings along the north bank of the river.

White Cross Ward. From The Low, where the White Cross stood, along Pickard's Lane (modern Chapel Road) as far as the pond in the Old Market and its western and northern sides.

Old Market Ward. The eastern side of the Old Market, as far as the bridge.

Ship Lane Ward. From the bridge, along the quayside and Ship Lane (Hill St) as far as the grammar school and common hall.

New Market Ward. The rest of Ship Lane, the market place and the buildings on the north side of (the later named) High Street.

Mill Ward. This area is harder to define, as its original description used markers such as 'Richard Best's House', which is vague to say the least! However, Mill Ward is thought to have encompassed the area from the Wheat Sheaf Inn (now owned by J D Wetherspoon) to Mill Hill at the east end of Ship Lane.

Despite all the precautions, the plague reached Wisbech by 1586. It has to be wondered whether it arrived courtesy of the poor soul chosen to deliver the funds to Guyhirn.

The disease is believed now to have been another outbreak of Bubonic Plague, the same sickness as had been labelled the Black Death in earlier times. Originally brought to the country by fleas on black rats, its rapid spread through the human population is thought to have been aided by the bites of fleas living on humans. Up to a week following infection, victims experienced fever and vomiting, after which the dreaded swellings called buboes appeared in the groin, armpits or on the neck. Death usually followed swiftly, though a few hardy sufferers recovered.

Wisbech's ten men stepped up procedures in an attempt to control the spread of disease. Each of them became the superintendant of one of the ten wards. They then, under the direction of the magistrates, appointed a governor for each ward. The governors controlled the movement of people in and out of their wards and around the town. Each ward also had a watchman to look out for wrong-doers and a constable to make any necessary arrests.

All visitors to the town, especially anyone arriving surreptitiously, were immediately reported to the superintendant of the relevant ward, so that he could keep track of who was staying there.

Anyone with symptoms of the plague was immediately confined to their own home, provided they had someone to care for them. If living alone, they were sent to the pest house, as it was called, a building in Barton designated for the care of plague sufferers. At the time, this would have been far enough out of town to keep the sick away from the general population.

To provide aid for the sufferers in the pest house or in their own homes, money was collected from all townspeople able to contribute, then distributed as necessary by the town bailey.

Once a person showing symptoms of the plague was admitted to the pest house or confined at home, they were forbidden to see anyone outside. The door of the house was marked with a cross to warn others to stay away and avoid the risk of infection. Food and other necessities were left on the doorstep and deliveries were taken by horse and cart to the sick at Barton.

These precautions were no more than common sense, but not everyone obeyed the rules. The watchmen were kept busy with patrolling their wards to stop the sick wandering around and infecting others. Anyone refusing to do as he or she was told was arrested by the constable and taken to the house of correction.

Godfrey Smith and Robert Smythe, who showed no signs of sickness themselves, ignored all warnings and went to visit their ailing friends in the Barton pest house. After enjoying a good catch-up with them, the two men walked around the town, putting everyone they met at risk of infection. They were finally caught and sent to the house of correction. Robert Smythe refused to go quietly and was apparently very rude to the ward deputy, using, according to the nineteenth century historian William Watson, 'vile words'.

It is uncertain where the house of correction was at that time. The castle was being used as a gaol, but mainly for political prisoners (more about that later). By 1602, when the castle gaol had become dilapidated, a building close to the bridge on the southern bank of the river was in use as a house of correction. It could well be that the same building was already in use as a lock-up sixteen years earlier, at the time of the plague.

The tasks of the women paid to care for the sick at Barton included the wrapping of bodies ready for collection and burial. The dead were buried immediately, to reduce the risk of infection. Burials took place before sunrise or after sunset, when townsfolk were safe at home. If no one was available to carry the bodies to church, they were carried on a horse drawn sled.

The plague remained in Wisbech throughout the rest of 1586 and the whole of 1587. The number of burials recorded in 1587, at the height of the pestilence, was two hundred and six; more than double the figure for a 'normal' year.

Records from this time are quite sparse, but show good sense and organisation. The death rate could well have been much higher had the situation not been so well managed. By isolating the sick, the spread of infection was greatly reduced.

Though it is unfortunate that more is not known about Wisbech's fight against the plague, more detailed accounts have survived from nearby Holland in Lincolnshire. This information relates to an outbreak of the plague in 1636, but it is likely that at least some of Holland's precautions were also used fifty years earlier in Wisbech.

In Lincolnshire, for example, watchmen were fined three shillings and four pence or risked three days' imprisonment if they failed in their duty to keep a close watch on their ward.

All dogs and cats had to be kept indoors or securely chained at all times to stop them wandering about and spreading disease. If any poor creature found its way outside and was reported, it was killed and its body burned. The animal's owner was fined two pence.

All bakers, butchers and other suppliers of food had to move their businesses out of the worst affected areas to a safer part of town. This was to keep food free of infection.

Everyone involved in the care of the sick had to carry a white stick to warn others of the risk of disease. White sticks were also carried by patients recovering from the plague. They were ordered to stay away from others for six weeks after the last of their symptoms had disappeared.

Any inn or alehouse blighted by sickness had to have its sign taken down and cease trading for the duration. A cross was painted on the door, as with any other building housing the sick.

Any weddings, baptisms or burials were to be attended by no greater number of people than was strictly necessary.

No fairs were allowed, since travelling tradespeople were a risk to the spread of disease over a wider area. Even the weekly market was allowed only in areas of town deemed to be safe.

All bedding and clothing which had been used by the dead had to be aired or burned. Justices of the Peace could allow recompense for this financial loss if necessary. This rule is known to have been enforced in Wisbech.

In September 1587 Edward Wright was reported for throwing dirty, infected clothes into the Nene, rather than airing or burning them. He was duly sent to the house of correction.

By that November, a system was in place to pay a regular weekly allowance to the sick. The end was at last in sight.

As people began to recover from their symptoms, they were assessed and their ward governor decided how soon they would be able to leave their homes and how far they could go. They were still not permitted to enter other houses and were fined if they did so.

At the end of that same month, the governors allowed nine people to leave the pest house at Barton, paying them twelve pence each to help them return to their everyday lives. Others, who had disobeyed orders, were punished. One was put in the town stocks and another tied to a post of the market cross and given twenty lashings of the whip.

On the third of December the governors allowed the remaining eleven pest house patients to go home. They were ordered to remain indoors and, even when eventually allowed to attend church services, had to sit apart from everyone else.

The ward superintendants and governors continued to regulate with caution. As Christmas approached, they came up with a plan to stop the poor begging from door to door, an old custom which would have risked the spread of any remaining infection. To avoid the need for begging, each governor made a list of everyone in his ward willing to donate to the needy. A second list was drawn up of those in need and the donations were distributed accordingly. For the Christmas of 1587 begging was both forbidden and unnecessary.

Despite signs that the plague was gradually receding from Wisbech, the disease clung on to claim both rich and poor. Robert Scotred, the governor of Barton Ward, succumbed to the pestilence in December.

As the new year of 1588 began, the plague was definitely on its way out, but any remaining cases were still carefully policed. In January, a shopkeeper called James Gooderricke was suspected of having plague symptoms. He must have been reluctant to cease trading because he was threatened with the house of correction if he didn't shut his shop, stay inside and stop receiving visitors. It seems he behaved himself in the end, because in April the corporation advanced him a loan of five pounds to help him rebuild his business.

That same April a couple by the name of Hervye, who had also recovered from the plague, was ordered to remove the goods from their house and lay them out to air by the river. They then had to light a fire in the house, presumably to fumigate it.

In 1588 the number of burials in Wisbech dropped to a far more normal ninety-seven.

Outbreaks of the plague continued to occur in the Fens throughout the 1580s and the next century, though Wisbech was spared further visitations. Even the well documented London plague of 1665 failed to spread to Wisbech, though it reached Ramsey in 1666. It hit the Fenland town badly, the number of victims too great for the authorities to cope with. Some bodies never even made it to the church. In July, Elizabeth, the wife of Thomas Middleton, was buried in her own garden.

Life in Wisbech gradually returned to normal during the early months of 1588. Then, one April midnight, a fire broke out in the Old Market. It must have been alarming enough to earn itself a mention in town records, but it was hardly in the same league as the Great Fire of London. It had a similarly cleansing effect, though, coming as it did straight after the plague and fumigating the alleyways of the Old Market that ran down to the river.

The fire clearly wasn't severe enough to excuse Wisbech from paying its ship money.

The threat of war with Spain was looming ever larger and Protestant England was vulnerable against the Catholic powers of Europe backed by the Pope. England needed to build warships to fight the mighty Spanish Armada when it arrived, and she needed to build them quickly. The government's coffers were close to empty, however, and so ship money had to be raised from the country.

The names of local subscribers, each of whom contributed the considerable sum of £25, are still there in the records. William Scotred, William Sturmyn, James Sallibanke, Robert Lyne and Robert Cowper were all Wisbech men. Contributing the same amount were Thomas Phage of March, Edmund Laverocke of Upwell, and Thomas Jones of Leverington.

Fortunately their money did not go to waste. In 1588, the great Armada was defeated by the smaller English ships and England was spared invasion as well as, no doubt, yet another religious upheaval.

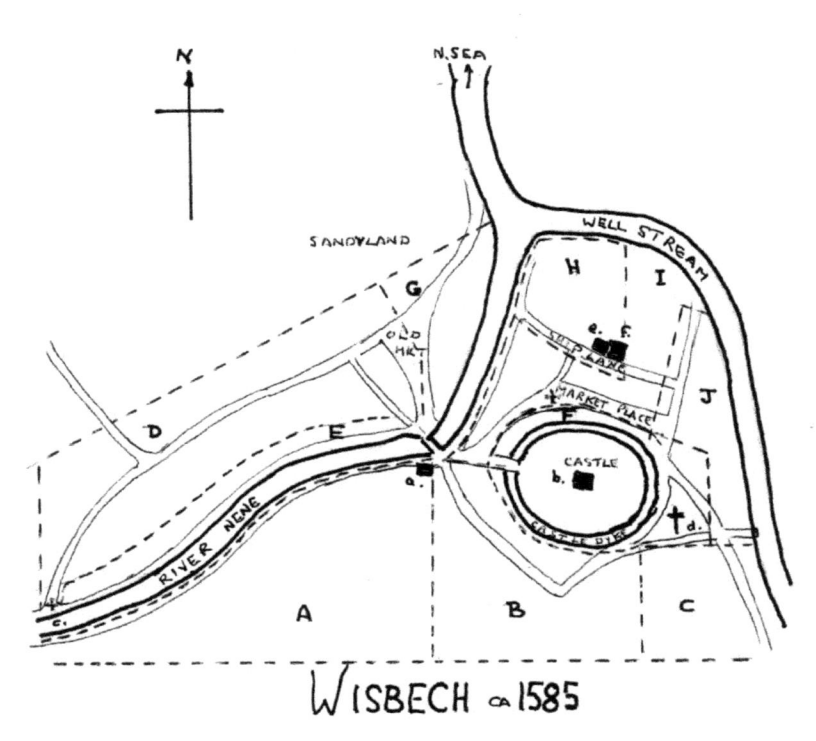

WISBECH c.1585

WARDS
A. SOUTH
B. CASTLE
C. TIMBER
D. WHITE CROSS
E. BARTON
F. CHURCH
G. OLD MARKET
H. SHIP LANE
I. NEW MARKET
J. MILL

LANDMARKS
a. HOUSE OF CORRECTIONS
b. CASTLE
c. WHITE CROSS OF THE LOW
d. ST. PETER AND ST. PAUL'S
e. GRAMMAR SCHOOL
f. COMMON HALL

Sketch map of Wisbech c.1585 with wards

Goings-On at the Castle

Wisbech Castle, with its law courts and prison, had always been a powerful presence at the centre of town. Though rebuilt in brick and perhaps less menacing to the eye than the original Norman fortress of stone, it remained the focus of justice and authority, as well as housing the Bishop of Ely when in town.

An article in the Victorian magazine, Fenland Notes and Queries, quotes a source from 1577 which tells of complaints received by Bishop Richard Cox about 'lettinge Wisbitche Castell utterly to goe to ruinne and pullyng downe and selling all the leade and timber of the keepe of the said castell.'

Responding to the complaint, the bishop pointed out that the only demolition to have taken place had been inside an ancient round tower. (This probably remained from the original Norman structure). The tower which stood in the castle yard, the bishop went on to explain, had once been used as a lodging, but had become so dilapidated that no one dared to enter it any more. He had been advised to pull down its inner walls, leaving the outer shell standing. The money raised from the sale of reclaimed materials had gone towards the repair of the three mile long damaged river bank at Waldersea. He had also added money from his own purse to have the work completed.

That told them! The bishop's critic was presumably satisfied, because no more was said on the matter.

The castle was about to take centre stage again in the town's history. Its gaol, having been the holding place for the Protestant Wisbech Martyrs in Queen Mary's time, now became a prison for Catholics.

Queen Elizabeth did not set out to persecute Catholics, having a more tolerant attitude to religious practice than her forebears, but her fear of Catholic plots was becoming stronger. Anyone seen as a threat to her or her government was imprisoned.

The individuals held on charge of conspiracy in Wisbech in the 1580s included two former Catholic bishops of Lincoln, Thomas Whyte and Thomas Watson. Bishop Watson had become the Bishop of Lincoln during Queen Mary's reign. He had managed to recover many of the Church's possessions lost under Henry VIII and Edward VI, including vestments, furniture, plate and even whole estates. But then, under the new Protestant Queen Elizabeth he found himself distinctly out of favour. He was imprisoned in London for twenty years before being moved to Wisbech, where he died in 1584. He was buried in St Peter's churchyard, close to the castle walls.

Another prisoner who died at the castle was John de Feckenham. He had endured a lifetime of difficulties. His open disapproval of the Reforms of Henry VIII and Edward VI had earned him imprisonment in the Tower of London. Life had improved greatly for him during the next reign, when he had become Queen Mary's private confessor, the Dean of St Paul's Cathedral and the Abbot of Westminster. Sadly, this was but a short reprieve. He was to be the last Abbot of Westminster.

The young Queen Elizabeth, however, was willing to keep him in a prominent position in her Church. This was on the condition that he signed the Oath of Supremacy, accepting her as head of the English Church. He refused and was therefore obliged to spend the next twenty-three years in prison, first in the grim Tower of London, then in the gloom of Wisbech Castle.

John de Feckenham died there in 1585, the year before the plague came to town. He was buried in St Peter's churchyard, but not before he had carried out a number of good deeds for the local area. Though his accommodation at Wisbech Castle can't have been very comfortable, he must have had a degree of freedom within its walls. He took an interest in the town, paying for work on the stone market cross and funding the building of a road across the Fens, later to be known as 'Fecknam's Way'.

By 1585 English Catholics were being watched. Though they risked being reported by government informers, many Catholic families were continuing to attend Mass in their own homes.

A new bill, the Bond of Association, brought in harsh new measures. Any seminary priests or Jesuits who had joined the priesthood since the beginning of Elizabeth's reign were given forty days to leave the country. If they refused and stayed on in secret they risked terrible punishment, but still some chose to do this. Constantly evading the authorities and hiding in deviously constructed priest holes within the walls and floors of large houses, many were caught and charged with treason. This crime was punished by the grisly death sentence of hanging, drawing and quartering.

Some priests and secular Catholics were not considered dangerous as such, but were seen as an undesirable influence on others. These individuals were confined in Wisbech Castle or similarly secure places, to keep them quiet. Others, usually men without formal education who just stirred up unrest and made a nuisance of themselves, were banished from the country and threatened with execution if they returned.

During the 1580s and 90s around fifteen hundred Catholic priests were sent to prisons like Banbury and Wisbech on suspicion of conspiracy. Despite the efforts of Protestant churchmen, the Catholics refused to recant, even to discuss their faith with preachers of the Reformed Church.

Bishop Cox of Ely despaired at his failure, and that of his clergy, to make the prisoners see sense. One particular group of priests had refused to talk to Dr Fulke, a Fellow of St John's, Cambridge. Reluctantly, the bishop had to give up with them, referring them to an assembly at Wisbech Castle. Apparently, they were sent by 'a secret way', to keep them away from the townspeople. It was a well kept secret; no clues remain as to its whereabouts.

Some castle prisoners were to become notorious, even household names.

While England was bracing itself for the arrival of the Spanish Armada, defeat by Catholic Spain was a real threat and the fear of Catholic plots intensified. In 1588 Robert Catesby and Francis Tresham were among a number of Catholics sent to Wisbech Castle. Their fervent beliefs and idealism were seen as a threat to Queen Elizabeth's government. They were later released, but the suspicions about their activities were not misplaced. They would later become key players in the Gunpowder Plot against King James I.

Among the other prisoners at Wisbech Castle were Jesuits like Bishop William Weston, Christopher Holywood and Thomas Pounde. Jesuits were a Roman Catholic order of priests founded in 1534 to do missionary work. They displayed total obedience to the Pope, were fiercely opposed to the Reformation and underwent strict, military-style training.

William Weston had been held at the castle since 1577. He had been charged with a catalogue of offences; some true, some false and some downright silly. At his court hearing, he had argued so well against all of the charges that doubt was thrown even on the valid ones. One of the more fanciful accusations had been the use of witchcraft to cast out evil spirits. The charge had come about through reports of shrieking and howling heard during his services. Since members of the clergy were forbidden to use prayer to cast out devils without a license from the bishop, this accusation was fairly common against priests with papist leanings.

The castle became the enforced residence of many Jesuits, as well as other Catholics. Usually, there were between thirty and thirty-five prisoners held there at a time and in the early years the regime was a strict one. The prisoners were confined to their cells for most of the day and night, let out only for a little fresh air in the garden and to share meals at the common table.

These meals were attended by Edward Grey, the castle keeper who was also a Justice of the Peace. He sat at one end of the table while his wife positioned herself at the other, both of them watching for any misconduct.

The keeper had good reason to be careful, as it turned out. During his absence on one occasion, two of the prisoners, Charles Borne and Nicholas Scroope, beat his servants. As punishment, Borne was clapped in irons and Scroope was confined to his cell for ten days.

Conditions at the castle began to relax somewhat after the first three years or so. Dr Bagshawe, a Catholic priest held there for many years, wrote about the unity and brotherly kindness in which he and his fellow prisoners were allowed to live. For recreation, he said, they had a garden to walk in and they were even permitted to leave the castle on occasions to walk around the town. Their custom made them popular with Wisbech tradesmen and the alms they distributed among the needy made them beloved of the poor. Well wishers sent them money, wine and fine food, such as venison and spices, for their table. Father Bluet, affectionately known as Old Blue, was in charge of receiving these gifts and sharing them equally between the prisoners.

They no longer had to eat all their meals at the common table, having a kitchen in which their favourite dishes could be prepared. They were allowed to invite guests to dine and sup with them and were even allowed to keep servants. The castle began to resemble more a seminary college than a prison. An altar was set up in the castle vaults, Mass was celebrated as in the old days and there were lectures on Hebrew and Greek scriptures for them to attend.

Dr Bagshawe was well respected within the community and was chosen to take precedence at the high table in the hall when the community ate together. He was keen to make life as pleasant as possible, and to cheer things up at Christmas he introduced some traditional entertainment.

Most of the company welcomed his efforts and were happy when Dr Bagshawe and Father Bluet invited a group of Morris Men, complete with a Hobby Horse (a principal performer in Morris dances), to entertain them. But not everyone was pleased. The Jesuits saw such frivolity as sinful and during the Christmas festivities of 1595 they walked out of the hall in protest.

Just before this, the Jesuit Father Weston had been elected as head of the thirty-three strong community. This choice had not gone down well with the secular Catholics and the rift between the Jesuits and the others had begun to widen. The Christmas protest, therefore, did nothing to restore harmony in the community.

Having left the hall to show his objections, Father Weston retreated to his cell and remained there for two weeks, issuing orders and new sets of rules to the community. Fathers Bluet, Bagshawe and others objected to most of these commands and the situation grew steadily worse. William Medley, the castle keeper and Justice of the Peace who had replaced Edward Gray on his death, attempted to settle the dispute.

It was no easy task. As these troubles, later to be known as the 'Wisbech Stirs,' went on, eighteen Jesuits tried to make a separate community for themselves, but the lack of space made such a separation impractical, if not impossible.

Although William Medley achieved a tenuous reconciliation between the two factions, bitter disputes continued to break out for years. Mealtimes descended into chaos at times, pewter platters and other missiles being hurled about when things became really heated.

The year of 1595 was an especially troubled one for the community. Earlier in the year, the castle gatekeeper Edward Hall had been accused of involvement in strange secret practices with the prisoners. The accusation had come about through sounds overheard by the good folk of Wisbech as they passed the castle. Strange babbling noises were reported as coming from the castle hall at meal times.

Incredibly, this matter went as far as a court hearing, during which John Foxley, a Wisbech shoemaker, gave evidence. He said he had heard Master Wagg the butcher ask Edward Hall the keeper what all the strange noises were. Master Hall had been heard to explain that the babbling was merely Latin and that no more was uttered than would otherwise have been said in English. Presumably the charges were dropped after that, because nothing more was recorded on the matter.

Other outcomes, however, were more serious.

Back in the days of the keeper Edward Grey, two Wisbech brothers, Thomas and George Fisher, had been hired as castle servants. The boys had apparently enjoyed their work, serving and listening to the priests. In fact, they became so immersed in the teaching they received that they were practically converted to Catholicism.

Their real trouble began when they refused to attend services at their parish church, which of course was Protestant. They were warned by the authorities and told to turn up to church on a particular feast day to show their good intentions. The lads failed to attend. As their punishment, and to set an example to any other townspeople harbouring Catholic sentiments, the boys were taken to the market place and given a public flogging. They were then clapped in irons to send the message home.

For one of the boys, this rough justice only made him more determined. He ran away to Belgium to join other Catholics in Douay and later took holy orders.

The prisoners too were suffering, of course. Their long incarceration, however liberal the conditions, was detrimental to their mental health, as we would say now. A gaoler's report described the continuous sad lament of an inmate by the name of Browne. Locked in his cell at night, he complained bitterly about his parents being dead, his sister's indifference and his brother having sold off his land. He cried that he was weary of the Fens, with nothing to gaze at but the sky and the heron's morning flight from the uplands to the Wash.

The whole point of sending Catholics to prisons like Wisbech was that they would be forgotten and their influence would fail to spread, but it didn't always work like that. Many of the prisoners had become very popular with the townspeople. Such a situation was frowned on by the authorities, so after a while some of the inmates were moved to Framlingham Castle. One of them was 'Old Blue', Father Bluet. As the beloved priest was led away in fetters, the townspeople gathered to bid him a sad farewell.

The castle continued as a gaol for many years, receiving priests and lay Catholics from other prisons around the country until the early 1600s.

The town's ten wards continued to operate for years after the plague had died out, perhaps as a precaution against any recurrence. Governors remained in charge of their wards and in 1595 a new task was added to their list of responsibilities. From then on, each Sunday after evening prayer, they had to check and report on the need for poor relief within their ward. If for any reason they failed to send their weekly report, they were fined four pence.

The way in which the ten wards were laid out provides a useful guide to Wisbech at the end of the sixteenth century. By filling in the blanks from other sources, a picture emerges of how the town had developed since the beginning of the Tudor period.

The most obvious change was in the centre of town. A new butchers' shambles had been built in 1588 at the eastern end of the market place. Constructed just after the plague had left town, at a cost of £85.19s.4d, the shambles are thought to have been of oak. Fastened to the front of the building was a wood carving of a man felling an ox, a street sign showing the shambles' butchery role at a time when most people could neither read nor write. The upper floor was used for the storage of grain or flour and the ground floor was left open to the elements. Here, between the pillars which supported the building, butchers set out their meat for sale on stalls rented from the corporation.

There are various theories about the origin of the word 'shambles'. One likely source is from the Old English 'sceamel' for a stool or bench. The bench gradually evolved into a table or stall for the displaying and selling of meat.

A market cross had stood at the opposite end of the market place since at least the mid 1500s. It had been repaired a few times and had been used many times for public floggings. Despite this function, like similar structures in other towns, the cross was meant to remind the townspeople of their religious duty and to encourage honest dealings.

The market place would have been constantly busy by day. Shops, workshops and inns still filled the plots between the castle dyke and the square and around the market place itself. A great variety of trades were plied there; brewers, butchers, bakers, tanners, smiths, cobblers, candle makers, tailors, basket makers, fullers, weavers, barbers, and mercers were just some of the trades regularly mentioned in local court records.

Although the town's trade guilds kept a tight control of their own particular crafts, they were unable to prevent strangers coming into Wisbech on market day to sell their wares. Anyone could set up a stall on the Saturday market, so it was a good opportunity for local farmers' wives to sell their butter, cheese, eggs, poultry and milk.

Apart from during the plague years, an annual fair still came to town, bringing in travelling performers and purveyors of food, drink and all sorts of other goods.

All this activity created heavy wear and tear on the market place, but still it was resurfaced with little more than packed soil. Sometimes, as in 1549, rag stone was used to make a better surface, but this was far from being standard practice. In 1560, the level of the market place needed to be raised and soil was used from the river bank between Crabbe Marsh and Elm Leam. This presumably covered the old rag stone layer.

Another centre of activity, the Timber Market, with its warehouses and stacks of imported deals, or soft wood, that lined the bank of the old Well Stream, still marked the southern edge of Wisbech.

This part of town seems to have been little changed since the beginning of the century, but to the west there were signs of late Tudor development. The burgage plots lining the river banks in the Guyhirn direction were still mostly occupied by farm buildings, warehouses and cottages. To fit the narrow confines of the plots, some buildings were positioned side-on to the river, facing each other across narrow alleys or yards.

But now a few larger houses were appearing. Some of them faced the river and occupied the whole width of the plot. One of these, the handsome King's Hall, was built at the edge of town, in Barton Ward.

Detail from a painting in Peckover House showing King's Hall on North Brink (with permission of the National Trust Photo Library)

This grand Elizabethan home survived until the end of the eighteenth century before being demolished to make way for a more modern house. Fortunately, an image of King's Hall was captured shortly before its demise in a print of the riverside and the scene was later painted by FW Watts. The painting, which allows a rare glimpse of part of late Tudor Wisbech, has pride of place in the Breakfast Room of the National Trust's Peckover House.

The town was thriving and in 1592 the ten men of Wisbech purchased a portrait of Edward VI and hung it proudly in the common hall as a reminder of the king who had presented Wisbech with its charter.

The meticulous accounts kept by the ten men recorded all payments made by the corporation. These included the queen's tax and the wages paid to individuals such as the market watch, the brink watch and the churchwardens. It appears to have been at around this time that the word 'brink' began to be used for the town's river banks in the Barton and South wards. The names North and South

Brink as such, though, do not yet appear to have come into use.

However well the town was faring, there always seems to have been some kind of trouble for its ten men to sort out. In 1599 Wisbech was having trouble with its neighbours again. A dispute had broken out between Wisbech and Whittlesey over both towns' rights to Wisbech High Fen, which adjoined Whittlesey parish.

The problem was taken very seriously and a commission was raised in Chancery, ordering the corporation of Wisbech to deal with the matter. Frustratingly, as with so many references to disputes, the result was never recorded, but it must have been fairly quickly settled as it was not referred to again.

In some respects, the East of England seems to have been ahead of other regions. The 'Heames Black Book,' which commented on legal customs of the Isle of Ely, suggested that women were held in higher regard here than in other areas.

This view is supported by an entry in court records from 1595. Thomas Reson had gone to court demanding that John Hely grant a moiety (a half share) of a messuage in Wisbech to a certain unnamed widow. He declared that, according to the custom of the Wisbech Hundred, by ancient usage women who were dowable of tenements (widows) should be endowed with a moiety of that property.

Again, the outcome is unknown, but Thomas Reson was at least trying to stand up for the 'weaker sex'.

Though the prisoners of Wisbech Castle may not have agreed, the Elizabethan era had brought prosperity and stability for many. The combined effects of disease, flood and the general trend towards late marriage had reduced the population of Wisbech to 1,500 by the year 1600. With fewer mouths to feed, shortages were rarer and unemployment had fallen.

The queen had reached the end of her long reign and had no direct heirs. There must have been many who wondered how life would change when the new king, the queen's second cousin from Scotland, came to the throne.

They were about to find out.

CHAPTER FIVE

'Vast and Queachy Soyle'; James I and Charles I

The accession of James VI of Scotland to the English throne in 1603 created the union of Scotland and England. Wales had officially been incorporated as part of England in 1536 and as James I of England, the new king also inherited the Irish crown.

For the people of Fenland, James' reign would be one of relative stability. He would renew the town's charter and grant wider authority to the ten men. As a result, they would be able to purchase land, hold, sell and exchange estates on behalf of the corporate borough. They would even acquire new titles; for the first time the charter would refer to them as Capital Burgesses.

They were certainly never short of work. At a time when most of the country was talking about the failed Gunpowder Plot of November 1605, Wisbech's Capital Burgesses were busy with quite another matter.

In a small way, though, their problem was related to the national news. Robert Catesby and Francis Tresham, two of the Gunpowder Plot's conspirators, had been imprisoned in Wisbech Castle during the 1580s. Now, as they and their fellow conspirators met their fate, their old prison too gave up the ghost, so to speak.

The old castle had been deteriorating for years and had reached the stage where it was no longer fit for purpose. As a temporary solution, prisoners were sent to the gaol in

Ely, but transporting them back and forth to court in Wisbech was both impractical and expensive.

Wisbech needed a permanent gaol. As mentioned earlier, the burgesses had at some point begun to use two tenements close to the bridge on the south bank of the river as a house of correction. This building crops up in records in 1602, but it is possible that it had been in use as early as the plague years of the late 1580s. The corporation received eight pounds a year from the Isle of Ely to keep a gaol in Wisbech, but the building needed some work to make it more efficient. Accordingly, twelve thousand bricks were ordered in 1616 for the necessary improvements.

Door from the house of correction on South Brink (with permission of Wisbech and Fenland Museum)

Standing next door to the gaol on the south bank were four new almshouses. These had been gifted to the town in 1610 by a local benefactress, the widowed Mrs Sturmyn who had granted a hundred pounds to house aged and sick people.

At around the same time, a shire hall had been constructed on the market place, next to the shambles. The castle's old mote hall, which had housed the law courts since time immemorial, had by then fallen into disrepair, and so the new shire hall took over the role.

On its roof was a pillory. Wrong-doers spent long hours with their head and hands pushed through holes in the wooden frame of the pillory, the crowd below hurling rotten vegetables and other missiles at them, to add to their humiliation. For the punishment of more serious offences, a whipping post was installed behind the building.

The Bishop of Ely had not quite given up on the old castle, however. Dr Lancelot Andrew, the new bishop from 1609, spent around two thousand pounds on repairing it and other nearby residences. Even so, the castle by then was used for little more than providing accommodation for the bishop during his visits to Wisbech.

The town was gradually growing and evolving, new public buildings erected to serve specific purposes. In 1619, thanks to another of Mrs Sturmyn's legacies, a corn market house was built on the south-east side of the bridge, on the river bank, close to the gaol and the almshouses.

Wisbech still had its problems, of course. In 1607 another fire broke out in the Old Market, the flames making quick work of the dry timbers and thatch of the homes and businesses there. As before, though, the fire was contained before it spread too far.

Three years later, the burgesses of Wisbech found themselves in an even more worrying situation. They had purchased some land in Walpole, but their right to do so within the terms of the charter was questioned. Three of the Capital Burgesses were obliged to go to London, charter in hand, to seek advice. After a fair amount of argument, it seems the matter was resolved without any further trouble for the town.

But there was one problem which never went away, one which was discussed more and more as the new century wore on; flooding.

In 1604 the Wisbech Sewer Commission ordered a survey by Richard Atkins of Outwell. An eminent commissioner of sewers, he was very interested in the Fens. His survey, which was retained in the Sewer Commission's records, contains detailed description of the Fens before drainage, including an early mention of wind pumps.

When writing about south Cambridgeshire, he said it '...hath very good fens two miles broad and above a mile long, very meddowes within ye compasse whereof lye certen grounds of Sir William Hindes, where there is an Ingin or mill placed to cast water, and not far from thence another mill for ye towne, both serve to good purpose and empty ye water into a ditch which falleth into Willingham Mere....'

Windmills were gradually catching on. In 1610 farmers in Tydd St Giles applied to the commissioners for a mill to keep their land dry. Winter flooding affected them so badly that they regularly had to use boats to reach their cattle.

The farmers requested that the new windmill be paid for with taxes collected from all the local area's inhabitants, whether living on low ground, vulnerable to flooding, or on high. This didn't go down too well with folk living on higher ground, who saw no benefit in paying to keep someone else's land dry. In the end, the building of the mill went ahead, but the commissioners had to adjust the tax to make the scheme fair to all.

The seemingly never ending problems with drainage and navigation would not be resolved without large scale action, but the commissioners continued to do whatever they could on their own doorstep.

Navigation was still a problem for boats trying to reach the sea. This was not helped by the fact that the bed of the Wisbech Great River, as the Nene between Wisbech and the sea was called, was at a higher level than at Guyhirn. Thomas Nurrice, an elderly fisherman from Peterborough, was less than impressed with the state of affairs. He complained that, though he had no trouble getting from Guyhirn to Wisbech, between there and the sea his boat was frequently grounded because the river wasn't deep enough.

This obviously needed attention, but the Commission of Sewers had even more pressing problems. A new sluice was needed at the Horseshoe at Leverington. One had been built in 1571, but it must since have failed because in 1608 the commissioners decided that a new, strong sluice was required. This time, they were determined that it would be built to last.

The new sluice of brick and stone stood proudly for seven whole days. It was then swept away by the same high tides it had been built to resist. This must have been a real blow to the poor old commissioners, but they had to keep trying. A stone sluice at the Horseshoe was mentioned again in the 1630s, so they must have succeeded in the end.

In the meantime, they turned their attention to the river problem, but Thomas Nurrice and his fellow boatmen still had to wait until 1616 for something to be done. By then, he had probably retired. The bed of the Great River was eventually scoured out to a more practical depth and width. Work was also done to improve Morton's Leam and the river between Guyhirn and Wisbech.

The Shire Drain near Tydd St Giles also needed urgent attention. Although this drainage channel had decayed so badly that it was no longer effective, the people of Tydd were still being charged for its upkeep. Having to put up with a blocked ditch and floods, plus the taxes meant to prevent such problems, the people were very angry. Feelings exploded into a revolt and this at last prompted the commissioners to remedy the situation. In 1618 the Shire Drain was finally cleaned out and restored to its old depth and width.

The frustration and anger of the people of Tydd were based on genuine fear. Harsh winters were far more usual then, but some stood out as truly terrible, such as that of 1613 to 14. Memories of that year's violent storms, heavy snow and flooding must still have been fresh in the Tydd folks' minds, adding desperation to their revolt.

The impact of that winter on Wisbech and the surrounding Fenland was so profound that it was commemorated with a plaque in the south chancel of St Peter's Church. After little more than a century, the inscription was worn away and had become illegible, so the plaque was removed. Fortunately, some thoughtful person transcribed its wording and the nineteenth century historian, William Watson, quoted from it in his Wisbech history:

'....on the feast of All Saints, being the first of November in the year of Our Lord 1613, late in the night the sea broke in through the violence of a north-east wind meeting with a spring tide and overflowed all Marshland, with this town of Wisbech, both on the north side and the south, and almost the whole hundred round about to the great danger of men's lives and the loss of some. Besides the exceeding great loss which these countries sustained through the breach of banks and spoil of corn, cattle and housing, which could not be estimated....'

The transcription goes on to say that the heavy snow of the following January and February led to severe flooding when it melted. On the twenty-third of March the Eau Brink sea wall between Tydd St Giles and Spalding was overtopped and broken down in several places.

Catastrophes like these, through which many lost their lives and many others faced financial ruin, were of course nothing new. They had recurred with worrying regularity throughout the recorded history of the Fens.

For people living beyond the reaches of the towns there was no protection from what nature threw at them. Most chose to live on the Fenland 'islands' of higher ground, but even so their homes were frequently ankle deep in water.

Compensations for this hard life came mostly in the form of good hunting. A poem of 1622 named some of the birds which were regularly caught for food or sold to provide income. Ducks, mallards, widgeons, dab chicks, red shanks, geese, cranes, gulls, curlews, cormorants and ospreys were all mentioned. A much earlier publication, Piercy's Household Book of 1512, gave the price which some of these birds were fetching at that time. Lapwings and dotterills were a penny each, though seagulls, plovers, woodcocks and redshanks cost a penny-halfpenny. Tern and snipe were the cheapest at three for a penny.

'Poly-Olbion' was another poem inspired by this wild and lonely region. Written in 1613 by Michael Drayton, this long work describes an imaginary journey through English and Welsh landscapes and includes a passage through the

Fens. Their watery nature clearly made a strong impression on the poet.

'Through quicksands, beach and Ouse, the Washes she must wade
Where Neptune every day doth powerfully invade.
The vast and queachy soyle, with Hosts of wallowing waves
From whose impetuous force, that who himselfe not saves.'

Drayton goes on to describe the irises, bulrushes and reeds that grew so profusely at the waters' edge, as well as peat cutting and the gathering of sedge and reeds for thatching. Then he talks about the wildfowler who '....over dykes upon his stilts doth walke....'

Other sources of information about the Fens before drainage are impossible to pin down to any one author. Some country practices have been passed down through so many generations that no one can be sure of where or when they originated. One of these is the use of marks to keep records.

Around the beginning of the 1600s there is said to have been a tavern on the north bank of Morton's Leam, between Stanground and Guyhirn, near a place called Cross Guns. It was a favourite haunt of fishermen and wildfowlers working on the washes and of lightermen whose barges carried timber and other cargo along the river from Wisbech to Northampton. Each of the tavern's regular customers had his own seat and his tab was marked on the wall above that place. Whenever he bought an ale, it was recorded with a horizontal line preceded by the letter Q for quart. A separate tobacco tally was shown by the letter T followed by horizontal lines in the same way.

A similar method was used to determine the pay due to labourers digging drains. Most of them were illiterate, so a simple square shape was drawn to indicate a day's work. Three sides of the square showed three quarters of a day, two sides half a day and a single line a quarter of a day.

Wherever the tavern's precise location, it was probably busier than usual on the day in 1623 when the English people heard that the heir to the throne had returned from Spain. Perhaps the fishermen and lightermen were as keen as the rest of the country to raise a cup to the health of the young Prince Charles.

If so, they were drinking to serious and fundamental change for the Fens, change which would eventually affect them all.

Charles I

Patriotic fervour filled the streets of Wisbech. Prince Charles, heir to the throne, had just returned from marriage negotiations in Spain and the nation was swept along on a tide of optimism. Bonfires were lit in the centre of Wisbech, ale and cakes were served in the streets and the church bells were rung in celebration. The bell ringing went on for so long, in fact, that the burgesses had to pay the ringers extra for their labours. Charles was so popular that two years later, in 1625 when he was crowned king, the town celebrated all over again.

Sadly, the country's enthusiasm did not last. The new king was indecisive, withdrawn and convinced of his divine right to rule. In his opinion, because he had been appointed to the task by God, he had no obligation to consult anyone, let alone parliament, about his decisions. This, and his involvement of the country in the Thirty Year's war in

Europe, with its huge loss of life, led to years of dissatisfaction and turmoil.

When arguments between the king and his government became too heated, he dissolved parliament and ruled without it for eleven years. His marriage to the Catholic Henrietta Maria made him even more unpopular, as fears of more religious upset were never far away.

Wisbech was not immune to the country's worries. Despite the prosperity of the town and port, the king's demand for ship money in 1634 came as a nasty surprise.

English kings had always been able to levy tax for the provision of ships without the consent of parliament, but this had applied only to times of war and was imposed only on ports and coastal towns. King Charles, however, was attempting to raise this money in peacetime. He was also including inland counties in his demands.

He sent an order to the sheriff of every English county to supply a ship of war, completely fitted out, for the king's service. Where it was impossible for a ship to be sailed to London, as from an inland region, the equivalent sum of money had to be raised and sent to the treasurer of the Navy, for his majesty's use.

The sheriffs of several inland counties, Warwickshire and Berkshire among them, protested vehemently and refused to collect the tax. The ports and coastal regions, however, had no way of getting out of it. The sheriffs of Norfolk and Cambridgeshire and the mayors of King's Lynn and Yarmouth met to decide on how much each area should contribute towards the £5,500 cost of a ship they had to supply.

Wisbech came out of the debate having to pay £340, a huge amount for a small town. The larger ports of King's

Lynn and Norwich, however, had even more to find, Lynn ending up with a bill for £1,192 and Norwich £1,601. Yarmouth contributed £940, while smaller towns were grouped together to raise their share. Thetford, Castle Rising and fifty-three small coastal villages clubbed together to raise £1,427.

The people of Wisbech were disgruntled to say the least and one of the Capital Burgesses went to London to plead exemption from the tax. He failed. He and all the other inhabitants of the town must have wondered why they'd spent so much on ale and cake to celebrate this king's coronation.

Purity and Charity

The number of Puritans in England had steadily been rising for decades. They had never been quiet about their dissatisfaction with Church Reforms, complaining that the work was incomplete. They were determined take things further and purify the Church of its old Catholic practices.

With their strict code of conduct and simple dress, their influence was felt everywhere. Even the Fenland town of Wisbech had its prominent Puritan families, two of which left impressive memorials behind them, so that their good deeds and sound principles would be remembered long after they had gone.

A rather magnificent memorial to Matthias and Jane Taylor has pride of place on the wall of the north chancel of St Peter and St Paul's Church. Matthias, who died at the age of sixty-seven on the second of February 1633, is shown kneeling in prayer with his wife Jane. Modelled in high relief, the Taylors are dressed in the expensively black dyed but simply styled clothes of successful middle class Puritans. Having trained in the family business as a linen dealer, Matthias went on to serve at various times as a Capital Burgess, the High Sheriff of Cambridgeshire and the Constable of the castle. For the last twenty years of his life he served as a Justice of the Peace.

The Parke memorial in St Peter's Church (with permission of the parish church)

Next to the Taylor memorial is an equally splendid one dedicated to Thomas Parke and his family. Like the Taylors, Thomas is depicted as kneeling in prayer with his then surviving widow Audrey, and wearing sober Puritan dress. Thomas died at the great age of eighty-seven on the first of January 1630, having enjoyed considerable success and having served as both Justice of the Peace in the Isle of Ely and the High Sheriff of Cambridgeshire and Huntingdonshire.

The Parkes did a lot for the town. In his Last Will and Testament, Thomas left twenty-eight acres of land in Elm, the income from which was used to boost the schoolmaster's wages. He also donated a hundred marks (about £70) for improvements to the highway between Wisbech and King's Lynn. His house, which was at the river end of Ship Lane, was left to the borough of Wisbech to provide shoes and stockings for the poor of the parish forever. Though his legacy didn't last quite that long, it continued to help the poor for many years.

Thomas Parke's generosity was not restricted to Wisbech. He founded four fellowships of sixteen pounds each a year, and four scholarships of ten pounds each a year at Peterhouse College, Cambridge. To fund all of this, land and tenements in Wisbech, Leverington, Guyhirn and Elm were conveyed to the college.

In 1639 Thomas' widow Audrey donated five acres of land in Wisbech, the rental income from which paid for a church sermon each year on the second of November. Any money left over provided cloth to make gowns for three poor women of the town. Rent from a further fifteen acres of land in Emneth paid for sermons on saints' days.

At a time when the gap between rich and poor was so great, such generosity and community spirit made a big difference. In 1626 William Scotred gifted by deed twelve acres of pasture in Wisbech St Mary, the rent from which was paid yearly to the churchwardens of St Peter's in Wisbech, to be distributed to the parish's most needy.

William Holmes was another generous benefactor. In his Will of 1656 he left land to support scholars both at Wisbech Grammar School and Cambridge University. He also left a fund of two hundred pounds to be paid in interest-free loans of ten pounds over three years to poor tradesmen in the town.

Another name recorded for posterity on a town memorial is that of Dr Henry Hawkins. On his death in 1631 he left three hundred pounds to build new almshouses. These homes, which housed six poor families, were erected on the south-east side of the parish church. When they eventually fell into disrepair and had to be replaced, Dr Hawkins' generosity was not forgotten. His memorial of 1631 was later reproduced and now hangs in the entrance to the flats at King John's House.

Later engraving of a plaque dated 1632 from Dr Hawkins' alms houses

The Matter of the Fens

The Fens, whether regarding their benefits or their shortcomings, were frequently under discussion. In 1628 a warrant was granted to Christopher Walton, allowing him to take partridges and other game birds, using nets and trammels, from Holland in Lincolnshire and from Marshland. He took these game birds to be kept near Royston and Newmarket, so that they could be hunted at his majesty's pleasure.

What was more often discussed, though, was the great potential of the Fens if they could be properly drained. There had been numerous schemes over the centuries, most of which had been successful for a while, but had improved small areas only and hadn't affected the Fens as a whole.

The Fens were increasingly regarded as a potential resource which was being wasted. To anyone whose livelihood did not depend on them, the Fens were nothing but 'a wilderness of stagnant pools', as the nineteenth century historian William Watson described them.

If properly drained, it was argued, they would become a valuable asset to the crown. King Charles was listening. He was the first monarch to show any real interest in the idea and at last it had royal backing.

Sir Cornelius Vermuyden came over from Holland in around 1629 and was contracted to drain the 'Great Level of the Fens'. He had already enjoyed considerable success in draining low lying regions of his own country, but despite his experience the Fenmen took an instant dislike to him. They had always instinctively distrusted incomers and were reluctant to work with this Dutchman.

To get round this problem, a local man was needed to work alongside Vermuyden, one who would inspire trust in the locals. The Commission of Sewers appointed Francis Russell, fourth Earl of Bedford, to the task. The Great Level, the area designated for drainage, would later be renamed the Bedford Level in the earl's honour.

The cost of such an enormous project, however, was too high even for the wealthy Earl of Bedford. In 1631 he gathered together a number of men who were willing to invest in the scheme with him. These men became known as the Adventurers.

The earl and Adventurers were to be rewarded for their investment with a share of the newly drained land. There are conflicting accounts about how the reclaimed land was to be divided, but according to one version, of the 95,000 acres to be drained, 12,000 were to go to the king. His majesty was already drawing up ambitious plans to develop his share. He had decided to build a new town near Manea and to call it Charlemont in his own honour.

His plans never materialised, presumably due to the problems he later encountered in fighting for his crown and his life.

A further 40,000 acres would be divided between the investors, leaving 43,000 acres to be set aside. The revenue from these 43,000 acres was designated to fund the future maintenance of all new ditches and banks. This agreement was finalised at a sitting of the Commission of Sewers on the thirteenth of January 1630 and was called the Lynn Law.

In 1634 King Charles I granted a charter of incorporation to the Earl of Bedford and the Adventurers. And so the work began.

The key element of Vermuyden's scheme was the straightening of existing rivers and the digging of new cuts, enabling water to run out to sea more efficiently. Existing river banks would be reinforced.

His aim was to keep the land dry in summer, allowing crops to be grown without the danger of flooding. His scheme could not prevent winter flooding, however, so Vermuyden was making no promises about year-round flood prevention at this stage.

For the next few years, the gruelling digging of new drains and banks and the straightening of rivers went on. Several new channels were created, including Bevill's Leam, between Whittlesey Mere and Guyhirn, and the ten mile long Peakirk Drain between Peterborough Great Fen and Guyhirn. (This ran roughly along the route of the modern A47). A new sluice on the Well Creek near Outwell was also built.

The huge amount of labour involved in this scheme would have been bad enough, even without interference from the locals. To most Fen people, the work meant nothing but bad news. Through countless generations, they had adapted to their damp and difficult environment. They knew how to cope with its many hardships and had learned to make the most of its resources. Drainage would alter their land completely and forever, threatening the only way of life they knew. They also faced the loss of their common rights.

Once areas of the Fen were drained and allocated to investors, they would be fenced off and made out of bounds to the locals. This would be the very same common land on which they had always hunted, fished and gathered reeds, sedge and willow.

The Fen people saw this coming and they didn't just grumble; they acted. They attacked the newly dug cuts and embankments, damaged river banks and set fire to freshly built wooden sluices. Some of their actions, though, misfired and harmed local people. Their vandalism created sudden and serious floods which on more than one occasion led to people drowning in their beds.

In a previous book, 'A Georgian House on the Brink', I quoted a few lines from an old poem, 'The Powte's Complaint'. Its unknown poet could foresee an end to traditional ways of getting about in boats, on skates (skatches) and on stilts. He knew that the landscape he loved would soon become fields for incomers' crops and grass for their cattle. The frustration, bitterness and fear felt by the Fen people is so evident, that another verse just has to be put in here.

'Away with boats and rudder, farewell both boots and skatches,
No need of one nor t'other, men now make better matches;
Stilt-makers all and tanners shall complain of this disaster,
For they will make each muddy lake for Essex calves a pasture.'

The Fenmen continued to make trouble for years and were more than ready to oppose the law. In 1637 a group of messengers from the Star Chamber, the court of law at Westminster, arrived in the area on official business. They were met by Peter Jarvis, the local constable, who warned them not to venture into Wicken Fen. The people there, he explained, together with folk from Soham, Barrack and Topham, were preparing to riot.

Disregarding such a puny threat from a few peasants with pitchforks, the London messengers rode fearlessly into Wicken Fen. They soon encountered the mob they had been warned about. The messengers tried to assert their authority by charging John Moredack, one of the mob's most belligerent members, to obey the council's warrant. As they approached him, however, John pushed them away with a pike. The women moved in, throwing stones and hurling abuse at their unwanted visitors and, taking one last look at so many pitchforks raised in anger, the messengers beat a swift retreat.

In the same year rebellions broke out at Holme and Wereham, in which banks and fences along newly cut ditches were badly damaged. The authorities were determined to track down the vandals. They had to use a boat to reach some of the culprits' houses, in one of which lived an old woman said to be a witch. As the boat neared her house, one of the watermen was stricken by a severe crick in his back. Ignorance and fear of witchcraft being what it was, the man assumed he'd been cursed. On the twenty-fifth of May the poor woman was taken away and imprisoned in Wisbech gaol.

Meanwhile, work carried out closer to home resulted in an interesting discovery.

In 1636, the River Nene between Guyhirn and Wisbech was being scoured out and deepened. The workmen had reached a level of eight feet beneath the old river bed when they discovered a stony layer. Lying on this gravel were several ancient boats.

Unfortunately, there was no method then for dating finds such as this, but the workmen knew they had discovered an earlier river bed dating from one of the waterway's busier periods. As well as emphasising the effect of silt on rivers, the find was a reminder of how long that waterway, once known as the Wysbeck, had been in use.

In the town itself, Wisbech Town Bridge was yet again in need of repair. Back in 1612, things had really been allowed to get out of hand. The corporate borough had been indicted for failing to repair the bridge, resulting in a fine and hasty repairs. By 1637 the structure was weakening again, but this time the burgesses were better organised, appointing surveyors to assess the job and carrying out the necessary work more efficiently.

That same year, on the twelfth of October 1637, the Commission of Sewers declared Vermuyden's drainage work completed, according to Lynn Law.

The promised acres were duly handed over to the Adventurers and the Earl of Bedford and, for a few weeks at least, everything must have seemed rosy.

Until the king's next move.

Without the consent of parliament, Charles had decided to levy a huge tax on the investors' new land. This was very bad news indeed. The unexpected tax, added to the heavy sums already invested, was the last financial straw for many of them. Underestimated costs, and having to repair damage inflicted by rebellious Fenmen, meant that even before the tax many Adventurers faced bankruptcy. The wealthy Earl of Bedford was one of the few who remained solvent.

To make matters even worse, harvests in the early years following drainage were poor. The first winter's heavy snow and rain, which went on long into the growing season, left the land under water again.

This didn't mean that Vermuyden's scheme had failed. After all, he had only promised to prevent flooding in summer, but understanding this did not help matters.

Things were not going well for the king, either. Unsurprisingly, parliament objected to his raising of taxes without their consent. The king's dogged belief in his divine right to rule, and basically to do what he liked without having to consult anyone, was causing a severe rift.

The simmering resentment between the king and his parliament eventually boiled over into civil war. This long, bitter armed conflict between the parliamentarians (known as Roundheads because of their severe haircuts) and the royalists (known as Cavaliers because of their flamboyant appearance) divided the English people. It created rifts in families, towns and social classes and dragged on from 1642 to 1651.

Many parliamentarians were Puritans. Their open disapproval of the established Church, with the king at its head and the tithes which made the poor even poorer, meant that anyone with Puritan leanings was naturally opposed to the crown.

The name of Oliver Cromwell was heard more and more. Born in Huntingdon and loyal to the parliamentary side, he was already the town's Member of Parliament and his star was steadily rising. He was very popular in Wisbech and the Isle of Ely and was soon appointed as governor for the Isle.

Wisbech was garrisoned for parliament before long. Fortifications were added to the old castle and an outpost was established a mile downstream at the Horseshoe, close to the Lincolnshire border. The soldiers stationed there were under the command of Colonel Sir John Palgrave and Captain William Dodson and were tasked with securing the road out of royalist Lincolnshire. This defence did not come cheaply for Wisbech. The Capital Burgesses were obliged to advance the colonel the mighty sum of £150 to cover his costs and a further £11.12s.6d for the castle's new defences.

Cromwell's first official visits to the Fens were an enormous success. He was so well received by the Fenmen that they hailed him Lord of the Fens.

One of his earliest visits took place in November 1642. When he first arrived, he stood in what appeared to be the middle of nowhere, an apparently uninhabited watery wasteland. The recently constructed banks and drains were already in a state of neglect; war had taken priority over maintenance and water was reclaiming the land.

Within minutes of his arrival, people began to appear. As if from nowhere, they came in their hundreds to greet him. It wasn't just the ordinary folk who gathered. There were also men who had invested in the drainage scheme and who faced ruin. They despaired of the king and his taxes and felt he had broken faith with them.

United in disillusionment, Fen men and women were pinning their hopes on the new governor of the Isle of Ely. Cromwell knew just what to say to eases their worries. He told the investors not to pay a penny of the tax until they knew the outcome of a legal battle that was going on at the time. A man called John Hampden had recently been charged for refusing to pay the king's ship money. Now that the king's authority was less certain, Hampden was expected to win his case. If he did so, a precedent would be set and the investors might manage to avoid their tax.

This sort of advice was bound to make Oliver Cromwell popular and loyalty towards him in the Fens was steadily growing. He had a reputation for caring for people under his protection. Later, when there were troops under his command, he would have an equal sense of responsibility towards them.

Wisbech and the Isle of Ely were mercifully far away from the main conflicts of the civil war, but no one could truly escape what was going on. With Wisbech garrisoned for parliament, soldiers would have filled the town and 'normal' life must have felt like a distant memory.

In 1643 Cromwell and his parliamentary forces were stationed in Peterborough while laying siege to Crowland. On the ninth of May, having taken the town, the troops marched on to Stamford. At this point, the action, though not quite on Wisbech's doorstep, must have felt uncomfortably close. And the financial costs kept piling up. As the war ground on, the Isle of Ely was ordered to pay parliament £250 for a troop of horse to defend the region.

By 1644, the Roundhead Earl of Manchester was in command of seven counties, including Cambridgeshire and the Isle of Ely. The county had to pay its share of costs and £783.15s was duly sent towards the upkeep of ten regiments of horse and ten of foot.

Memories of these times and of Cromwell's presence in the Fens lived on for many years. One particular memory, passed down through the generations, concerns the time when Cromwell had his headquarters in Emneth, at Nine Chimney House. As he moved with his troops around the Isle, he stayed at other places too and a visit he made to a house in Elm has become part of local history.

One night, Cromwell and his troops called at Needham Hall in Elm. The owner of the house, Master William Dow, offered his important guest his best bed, but Cromwell is said to have declined it. Apparently, he explained that he'd most likely spend the following night in an open field, so he could manage without the luxury of a bed that night too. He chose to sleep instead on the oak table downstairs. A few of his officers were provided with beds, but his troops lodged in the outbuildings.

Another memory survives from these times. When the historian William Watson was writing in 1827, he knew of people with passed-down family memories from the civil war. An old man was still living in Elm whose grandfather, it was said, had as a boy seen Cromwell and his troops marching along the avenue leading to Needham Hall. The elderly man must have missed out a generation or two from his calculation, but the way in which he related his ancestor's tale is interesting. As the seventeenth century lad had described seeing the troops, he had apparently said, 'while Cromwell was ransacking the Fens...'

Clearly, not everyone was a fan of Cromwell and the constant presence of his troops.

There were other signs that opinion was divided. During the early years of the war a local rebellion broke out. It must have been of some significance, because it took eight hundred of Colonel Saxers' men to control it. The Corporate Borough of Wisbech had to foot the bill for quartering these extra troops, all thirty-five shillings and sixpence of it.

In 1646, Edward Buckworth and other local men were fined for 'delinquency'. In other words, they were showing disrespect towards the parliamentary forces, but their behaviour can't have been all that bad because they were granted pardons soon afterwards.

The war was going well for the Roundheads. In 1645 the New Model Army had become established under the command of Sir Thomas Fairfax. Before this, as had always been the case in warfare, both sides had consisted of a collection of private armies loyal to local leaders. The New Model Army was quite different. It was a professionally trained, centralised force with discipline and efficiency which came to symbolise the parliamentary side. It was the forerunner of today's professional army.

Though the royalists were rapidly losing ground, the civil war staggered on. The defence of the Isle of Ely had to be kept up and by 1648 the Isle was having to pay £70 a week to keep its troop of sixty horse. This was perhaps considered a necessary evil while the war continued, but the financial burden would go on after the war, throughout the Commonwealth and until after the restoration of the monarchy. These payments were still being made as late as 1690.

There were other demands on the Isle of Ely. The war had created supply problems throughout the country and Londoners were running out of fuel for their fires. In 1644 the Commons ordered the formation of a committee to organise the provision and carriage of turf and peat from Wisbech and the Isle of Ely to London.

The civil war, with all its misery and bloodshed, finally reached its horrific climax. On the thirtieth of January 1649 Charles I was executed for treason. However strong the complaints about his qualities as a monarch, the killing of a king was shocking and disturbing to many people.

Without a king, the country became a republic. The united countries of England, Ireland and Scotland were known as the Commonwealth.

CHAPTER SIX

The Dry Land Smiles; The Protectorate

Wisbech and the Fens had been on the side of parliament during the war, so perhaps life in the Commonwealth, with the same officials in charge, didn't feel all that different.

Even the wearisome nine year war was not quite done with. Cromwell still had a rebellion to crush in Ireland and royalists to deal with in Scotland. The New Model Army was kept on, together with the navy, both of which meant continuing high levels of tax for the people.

Yet Cromwell's star rose even higher; he emerged from the war as the natural leader of the new order he had fought so hard to create. In 1653 he was installed as Lord Protector of the Commonwealth. From then on, Britain was referred to as a Protectorate.

Like many other parliamentarians, Oliver Cromwell was a Puritan. As such, he believed that strict adherence to the Bible was necessary to lead a good life. Hard work paved the path to heaven, and pointless entertainment was discouraged.

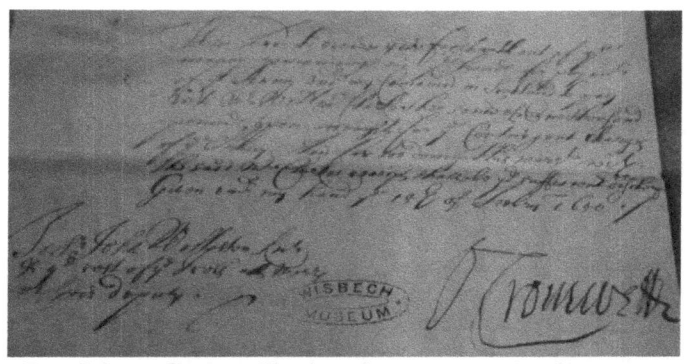

Detail from Cromwell's signed payment order for troops dated 31.12.1650 (with permission of Wisbech and Fenland Museum)

Many inns and taverns were shut down to discourage gatherings of individuals with royalist inclinations. Hotbeds of sinfulness, like race courses and theatres, were also closed. Drama and non-religious poetry were banned.

Wisbech folk are unlikely to have been bothered about the closure of theatres, since they'd never had one. Men and boys would, however, have missed their football. Football had been a favourite sport for centuries, played regularly after church on Sundays, but this too was prohibited. Blood sports, such as cock fighting and bear baiting were banned, which to modern thinking is a good thing, but to people living under the Protectorate it was just another unwelcome prohibition.

Soldiers were still stationed in Wisbech. As in other parts of the country, they made their presence keenly felt. They collected taxes and looked out for any undesirable behaviour, arresting anyone caught acting in a lewd manner or overheard swearing or blaspheming. Such miscreants were duly fined.

Even the celebration of Christmas was spoiled for most people. Both before and after Henry VIII's Reformation, feasting and merriment had played a strong role at Christmas, but such festivities were now firmly discouraged. The Puritan influence, now so strong in the country, dictated that Christmas was to be observed in a pious manner. Traditional decorations using holly and ivy were seen as wicked pagan symbols and so were banned.

Though reformed, the Church of England still encouraged too much ceremony for Puritan tastes. Churches were therefore stripped of any decoration that had survived previous purges. Even religious music and the singing of hymns were frowned on; Puritans believed that singing led to a dreamy state which was not conducive to listening to God's voice.

Ely Cathedral suffered a nasty dose of Puritan zeal and vandalism. In January 1644 soldiers ransacked the vestry and cloisters, making sure they smashed the cathedral's windows in the process.

Wisbech people could not ignore the new rules. Not only did they have the military breathing down their necks, but one of Lord Cromwell's right hand men was also living in their midst. The Right Honourable John Thurloe was not a native of Wisbech, but had made the town his home. Educated in the law, he had risen to become Cromwell's Secretary of State. He was also his spymaster.

Oliver Cromwell, despite his hard rule and Puritan convictions, promoted religious freedom. In this respect he was fair minded and considered that, since Puritans themselves were non-conformists, it was just to allow others to worship according to their conscience. He even allowed Jews, who had been expelled by King Edward I in 1290, to return to the country.

Unfortunately, Cromwell's parliament did not agree with all his views. They certainly did not support his religious tolerance. They voted to suppress all minority Puritan sects, such as Quakers, Levellers, Diggers and Ranters. Some of the more outspoken members of these sects found themselves in prison.

George Fox, the founder of the Quaker movement, was one of the more vehement non-conformists to be imprisoned. Perhaps out of curiosity, Lord Cromwell visited him in prison in 1655 and was so impressed with the man that he ordered his release. He gave him permission to address meetings anywhere in the Commonwealth.

Under Cromwell, attendance at Church of England services was not compulsory, nor was it a condition for entry into university, the professions or public office, as it had been for centuries. This change, in addition to the Puritan influence that was everywhere, greatly reduced the power of the established Church. Even marriage ceremonies could take place at other venues; a simple ceremony involving a Justice of the Peace was now a legal alternative.

The new order, unsurprisingly, was not to everyone's taste. A popular toast said to be drunk in private involved dropping a breadcrumb in a glass of wine. The glass was raised with the toast 'May Providence send this "crum-well" down!'

Another practice was to hold a glass of wine over a bowl of water on the table, thereby drinking to the king 'over the water'. They were referring to Charles, the exiled son of the late king who had fled the country in October 1651. Many secretly hoped for his return.

As the East Anglian people gradually grew used to life under the Protectorate, attention turned once more to the Fens.

A few years earlier, in 1647, heavy rain and high water had eroded the river banks protecting Wisbech, Elm, Upwell and Outwell. Fourteen thousand acres of land had suffered serious flooding, with the loss of many cattle and a good deal of corn and hay. It had been a disaster and the subject of drainage now returned to the top of the agenda.

There were, of course, many Fenlanders who must have hoped the subject of drainage had been dropped. They had enough trouble as it was, and it must have seemed as if their traditional way of life was forever under threat.

One such threat had come in 1649 to the people of Sutton in the Isle, near Ely. Ever since feudal times, a wide acreage of common land had been leased to feoffees (trustees) for the use of the people of the parish. Under this system, each person had a 'lot meadow.' Every year, before the hay was cut, the land was divided into lots using lock spits, or cuttings of sod at each end. This system had worked well for hundreds of years, each man having a fair share of land on which to graze his livestock and from which to collect hay.

But things had gone badly wrong for the villagers during the civil war. A few wealthy gentlemen of the parish had decided to donate four thousand acres of this common land to the Dean and Chapter of Ely Cathedral. Not only was this an outrageous betrayal of the ordinary parishioners and their needs, but questionable in law. The land didn't belong to these wealthy men to start with, so they had no right to give it away.

Fighting their case cannot have been easy for the people of Sutton in the Isle, but they sent an appeal to parliament. As usual, there is a lack of information in old records concerning the outcome, but perhaps no news is good news and it is to be hoped that justice prevailed.

Now drainage was being talked about again and even the Fenman's old ally was turning his back on them.

Oliver Cromwell, the man who had once been hailed as Lord of the Fens, the man who had seemed so understanding of the Fenlanders' fears, was now authorising a new phase of draining. The empathy he had shown now seemed little more than a political gesture, a clever trick to incite them further against their king.

Once more, Sir Cornelius Vermuyden was appointed, this time with the aid of William Russell, the son of the old Earl of Bedford.

As his father had done, William, the fifth Earl and first Duke of Bedford, gathered together a group of Adventurers. Once more, an agreement was reached to share out the reclaimed land when the work was completed. Since practically all the last Adventurers had been bankrupted by the scheme, the duke must have been one heck of a salesman to convince new investors to join in.

The second phase of work on the Great Level of the Fens aimed to prevent flooding both in winter and in summer. This was far more ambitious than the first phase, which had only aimed to prevent summer floods. There were hopes now that after drainage, crops such as coleseed (rape), wheat, hemp and flax would be grown more successfully.

The work would involve the construction of two new sluices, the Hermitage at Earith and one at Denver on the Ouse. More channels would also be cut, among them the Forty Foot Drain from Ramsey to Welches Dam, the Sixteen Foot Drain to Popham's Eau at Upwell (which drained the Central Fen around Chatteris and March) and a new channel to run parallel with Morton's Leam between Peterborough and Guyhirn.

In addition, natural rivers would be deepened and straightened, with new straight cuts bypassing bends and meanders. Watery landscapes, alive with iris, rustling reed beds and swaying grasses would give way to high banked channels cutting across dry fields. The loss of traditional Fenland, feared for so long, was becoming a reality. Agriculture would soon replace the old marshland economy.

The scheme was an impressive feat of civil engineering and one of its greatest challenges was finding a sufficiently large workforce. It was practically impossible to hire local labour, since Fen people were so fiercely opposed to drainage. Labour had to be brought in from outside. The Right Honourable John Thurloe suggested the drafting in of prisoners of war and putting them to work.

On the first of October 1651 a thousand Scottish prisoners of war, captured after the Battle of Dunbar in 1650, arrived in the Fens. Joining them were prisoners from the civil war Battle of Worcester and five hundred Dutch sailors captured during an engagement off Portland Bill.

There were other prisoners too, local men convicted for petty crimes. With the prisoners of war, they were set to work digging the many new drains and banks across Cambridgeshire, Huntingdonshire and Norfolk. Collectively, the workers were referred to as 'dykers' or 'fen dykers,' which is one possible origin of the term 'Fen Tigers'. Of course, it could equally be due to their general toughness and belligerence!

The prisoners worked with spades and shovels and used baskets to carry away the soil. They slept in rough huts which could be dismantled and moved along the banks as the work progressed. They endured long working hours in damp and miserable conditions with the ever present threat of malaria. The locals had become practically immune to this disease through years of living close to the stagnant ponds which were breeding grounds for malaria-carrying mosquitoes. The foreigners, however, stood no chance. Many of them became sick and many died.

And they had even more to put up with. The dykers suffered the abuse and vandalism of the local people who despised them for working on the scheme. This time, it wasn't just the freshly cut ditches and banks which were targeted; the workers themselves were attacked. In many cases they were badly injured and even killed.

The authorities seemed powerless to prevent the attacks. On the thirty-first of May 1653 a troop of horse had to be called in to sort out trouble between a local mob and dykers working on a piece of Adventurers' land. That same year, Thurloe himself had to deal with a particularly fierce riot. Eighty armed men from Swaffham and Bottisham had launched a night assault on a detachment of Colonel Humphrey's troops guarding a new section of drainage work.

The attacks just kept happening. Though punishments were harsh for protesters when finally caught, they were not easily put off. New trouble makers simply carried on where others had left off.

Revolts and vandalism were becoming more widespread, the authorities increasingly frustrated. A gentleman by the name of Anthony Hammond wrote to John Thurloe, expressing his doubts about the authorities' ability to deal with the unrest. The assize courts, still referred to by the old name of 'Oyer and Terminer', were not managing to deter offenders.

Yet, despite all the problems, by late 1652 the drainage of the Great (or Bedford) Level was completed. A service of thanksgiving was held in Ely Cathedral. For the individuals who had invested time and money in the project there must have been huge relief, but for others there was nothing but despair. Life for them would never be the same again.

A new authority, the Bedford Level Commission, was created in 1663 to look after the new system of drainage ditches, banks and sluices. To simplify administration, the Great Level was divided into three sections, the North, Middle and South Level Commissions.

The coat of arms of the Bedford Level Commission announced its confidence in the future with the motto, 'Arridet Aaridum' or 'The Dry Land Smiles.'

The Middle Level Commission maintained the area between Morton's Leam near Guyhirn and the New Bedford River, a stretch of land which included the Fens around Wisbech, March, Ramsey and Earith. It was responsible for all ditches, sluices and bridges, as well as the three hundred miles of river bank within its jurisdiction. The cost of keeping everything in good condition, both for navigation and drainage, was huge. Money had to be raised somehow.

History has a habit of repeating itself and once more taxation became the only viable option. Suddenly, the Adventurers were facing a large tax bill on their newly acquired land. The whole 95,000 acres were now to be taxed.

As before, this unexpected bill was the final blow for many Adventurers. Their costs had been enormous already, way beyond the sum expected to begin with. Few of them were able to pay the tax imposed by the Bedford

Level Commission, and even the wealthy Duke of Bedford was obliged to sell off property in order to pay his bills. His investment in drainage, together with that of his father, resulted in several of his manors in Devon having to be sold, as well as land in St Martin in the Fields.

Since most of the tax it charged was never paid, the Bedford Level Commission was nearly always short of money. The commissioners regularly had to rely on loans and it wasn't long before the necessary maintenance was falling behind and complaints were being received about localised flooding.

Yet somehow the system struggled along. To start with, there was cause for optimism. Crops such as flax, hemp, oats, wheat, woad, onions and peas were all successfully grown on the reclaimed land.

Meanwhile, life in Wisbech was beginning to settle down. The town bridge, which had borne the extra strain of civil war traffic, had to be repaired again at a cost of a hundred pounds, but otherwise things were peaceful enough.

Spreading out from the town were the cultivated fields of Sandyland to the north and along the river banks to the west. Little remains today of the farms or the buildings that went with them, but there are a few clues to give us an idea of life beside the river before its Brinks gained their Georgian good looks.

The Reed Barn at Peckover House (with permission of the National Trust)

One rare survivor is the Reed Barn, an attractive building in the grounds of the National Trust's Peckover House. It was built as a threshing barn in the mid 1600s and would have been one of several buildings serving a busy farm. The harvested wheat would have been taken to the barn to be flailed and winnowed to separate the grain from the chaff. The work was arduous and uncomfortable and created clouds of choking dust.

The barn has been well restored and thatched with Norfolk Reed. Its new role as a tea room and shop is a more tranquil one, preserving it to remind visitors of the rural life which once thrived on the outskirts of seventeenth century Wisbech.

Many folk in the town and surrounding countryside were living at subsistence level and relied on poor relief. Wealthy individuals continued to provide some support through legacies, one of whom was John Crane. He was a Cambridge apothecary who is thought to have been born in

Wisbech. He had supported local royalists at the end of the civil war and on his death in 1651 his legacies benefitted the people of four different towns.

He granted his Black Bull Inn messuage to help the people of Wisbech. Of this messuage, later known as the New Inn, one small building remains in New Inn Yard, between the river and market place. This black and white half timbered building is believed to have been used originally as stables and, apart from St Peter's Church, is the oldest building in Wisbech.

Half of the income from the Black Bull estate was used to give the school master of Wisbech Grammar School a pay rise. The other half provided corn and firewood for the poor at Christmas and was distributed each year on St Thomas' Day, December the twenty-first.

John Crane's executors were instructed to purchase land to yield sixty pounds a year. The first year, this income went to the University of Cambridge to support poor and sick scholars. The second year's revenue was paid as interest free, twenty year loans to young Wisbech men, to help set them up in business. The third year's income provided a similar facility for the youth of Cambridge, the fourth for King's Lynn and the fifth for Ipswich. In year six, the funding returned to Cambridge and the cycle was repeated throughout the years.

Any money left over each year went to relieve the poor imprisoned for debt. Others considered to be honest and godly, who had suffered a fall in fortune, could also benefit from Master Crane's legacy. He made it clear, however, that no money should go to 'dissembling, hypocritical persons.'

John Crane didn't stop there. He donated a hundred pounds for improvements to the common hall in Ship Lane where the Capital Burgesses held their meetings. The money was used to add a room on to the back of the grammar school next door, most likely to benefit both the hall and the school. The common hall continued to be used for town business until 1810.

Similarly, in 1656 Lord Viscount Saye and Sele left a hundred pounds to the Capital Burgesses to fund an annual donation to the poor at Christmas, to pay for clothing.

Despite such generosity, care for the poor suffered frequent setbacks. In 1651, a fire destroyed several dwellings on the south bank of the river, including the four almshouses built by Mrs Sturmyn.

Life under the Protectorate saw some startling changes. Some of them shook up local institutions and customs that had been in place for so long, they seemed to be set in stone.

The Manor of Wisbech, for example, had belonged since ancient times to the Church. Although much of the old Church owned land in the town had been sold off at the end of the fifteenth century, the manor was still a valuable asset.

With the established Church in a weakened state, the new authorities assumed the right to sell off Church property. And so the Manor of Wisbech went on to the market.

It was bought by Master Thomas Allen, Master Francis Rowland and others for the sum of £2,544.1s.6 ½d. We'd perhaps be forgiven for wondering what the halfpenny was for.

A separate large acreage of demesne land which had belonged to the Bishop of Ely since feudal times was sold to Master Jonathan Barnes and Master Richard Harrison for £1,915.16s.8d.

Wisbech Castle, which also belonged to the Church and had long since fallen into disrepair, was sold off too. Cromwell ordered it to be dismantled and in 1657 the site was sold to his Secretary of State, the Right Honourable John Thurloe.

Thurloe's new mansion soon rose from the rubble of the old castle. Following a design by Inigo Jones, it was very similar in appearance to Thorpe Hall in Longthorpe, Peterborough, the home of Cromwell's Lord Chief Justice, Oliver St John.

Thurloe's Mansion, from a model made by Peckover House volunteers in 2015 (with permission of the National Trust)

There was now a handsome new mansion at the centre of Wisbech. Where once had stood an austere Norman castle, replaced some four hundred years later by a brick-built Bishop's Palace, the graceful lines of a fashionable residence now dominated the town.

The old castle dyke was partially filled in and elegant gardens laid out. Just a few pools remained of the dyke, one of which was the cheerfully named Deadman's Pond in Deadman's Lane. This would survive until twentieth century development necessitated its removal.

Though a Regency villa, still known as Wisbech Castle, now occupies this principal plot in town, the vaults of Thurloe's Mansion can still be accessed from the garden. They continue to be a great source of speculation and mystery.

Branching off from the central passage are eight tunnels to the right and nine to the left, all constructed of brick. The ends of some of these tunnels are blocked off and one of them ends in what appears to be a bricked-up opening of some kind.

Theories abound about how these tunnels may have been used. Thurloe was Cromwell's spymaster as well as his Secretary of State. In the course of his work he and the officials working for him intercepted a great many messages and broke numerous codes, leading to the capture of enemies of state. The Well Stream formed the boundary with traditionally royalist Norfolk and it is speculated that the tunnels may have helped Thurloe's spying activities.

No one really knows, though. John Thurloe had a very short time to enjoy his mansion and any activity in the tunnels would quickly have come to an end.

There were other tunnels under Wisbech by this time, one under the market place, for example, and another near the Old Market. These were built for drainage.

John Thurloe ordered the construction of several drainage channels during his time in Wisbech. Amongst the brickwork of some of these old tunnels are a few red Tudor bricks. The red brick Bishops' Palace had only just been demolished, to clear the site for Thurloe's new mansion, so he would have had a lot of old bricks to dispose of. It is quite possible that some of them were recycled into the construction of drainage channels.

Even at that time, tunnels to aid drainage were not a new idea. According to the antiquarian Sir William Dugdale, there had been a brick pipe under the river near Wisbech as early as 1437. This had been used to take flood water from Elm under the Wisbech river and out to sea via Leverington. This enabled the excess water to by-pass the silted up port of Wisbech and lessen the risk of flooding to the town. Pretty ingenious for the fifteenth century!

Oliver Cromwell died in 1658, but John Thurloe suffered no drop in status. Cromwell was succeeded as Lord Protector by his son Richard, who relied heavily on the support of his father's secretary of state.

Thurloe became a Capital Burgess for Wisbech and was elected to represent the borough in parliament. This was a big step for Wisbech. Although the town had been a parliamentary borough since as early as 1300, it had never taken up the option to send a representative to parliament.

The sheriff of each county since early times had had to decide which of the towns within his county should be parliamentary boroughs. He had then to choose two citizens from each city and two burgesses from each borough, to be summoned to parliament. This system had been in use since at least 1298, during the reign of Edward I.

There was an exemption clause, however. If a borough couldn't afford to send burgesses to London, or if there was no one suitable for the task, the sheriff could excuse the borough from sending a representative.

Wisbech had always claimed exemption before, but at a meeting of Capital Burgesses in 1658, it was agreed that John Thurloe should have the honour of representing the borough in Richard Cromwell's parliament. There was a snag, however. Such was Thurloe's popularity that he had also been elected to represent the University of Cambridge, as well as the Borough of Huntingdon. In the end, he chose to represent the university, so Wisbech's plans were thwarted.

John Thurloe's decision did not lessen his generosity to Wisbech, where he would long be remembered as a liberal benefactor.

In 1658 he donated a hundred and fifty pounds to provide the town's poor children with apprenticeships. He also gave fifty pounds to construct a causeway (a raised bank with a path running along the top) from the Corn Market near the town bridge to the sluice down river.

He then spent a further fifty pounds on eighty-one books for the public library. The library was housed in the small room above the south porch of St Peter's Church which had been left vacant when the grammar school moved to new premises in Ship Lane. The collection of books had been growing slowly since 1654, when a number of burgesses had donated a few books. Thurloe's gift must have meant a huge improvement in the variety of books which could be borrowed by anyone able to read them.

Thurloe was honoured by the town for his good deeds when a wooden gallery was built for his private use on the southern side of St Peter's Church. He enjoyed great personal popularity in the town, but not everyone was impressed with the regime he represented.

In 1656 John Hobart and William Fisher signed a petition to parliament on behalf of the land owners and inhabitants of the Wisbech Hundred. This stated their objection to the level of tax they had been charged, which was significantly higher than in neighbouring areas. They demanded a tax refund of £2000 and exemption from arrears.

They were aggrieved that yet again they had major flood damage to deal with. The winter had been one of high rainfall and storms of such severity that the sea banks protecting Wisbech, Elm, Upwell and Outwell had given way. Homes, cattle, corn and hay had all been lost and the costs involved in putting right so much damage doubtless made the tax seem even more unreasonable. Whether the petition fell on deaf ears or was met with some success is not known.

The time of the Protectorate was drawing to a close. Richard Cromwell, even with the support of John Thurloe, lacked the steel and determination of his father. Before long, the regime was crumbling.

People were talking more and more of the king over the water.

CHAPTER SEVEN

'A Base Unwholesome Air'; Charles II and the Last Stuarts

In 1660 Charles II returned from exile and claimed the throne. The town bailiff announced the news to the people of Wisbech and the Capital Burgesses granted special funds so that the whole town could celebrate.

A wave of rejoicing swept through the nation. However well people had adjusted to life under Cromwell, many were heartily relieved to see an end to heavy restriction and sobriety.

There was at least one man in Wisbech, though, who greeted the news with caution. John Thurloe was arrested and accused of high treason. He survived, as it turned out, his skills and intelligence proving useful to the new king, but he lost his fine mansion in Wisbech. He moved to Lincolnshire, where he died suddenly in 1668 at the age of fifty-one. Despite his change in fortune, he continued to be remembered in Wisbech for his amiability and courtesy.

Thurloe's Mansion, or the 'castle', as all buildings occupying the site continued to be called, reverted to the See of Ely. With the restoration of the monarchy, all crown and Church property sold off during the Protectorate was restored to its original owners. This included all the Church land in Wisbech Manor which had been bought by local people.

For a few years, the Bishops of Ely went back to using the castle as their residence whenever they stayed in Wisbech. They lived well too, perhaps compensating for recent lean years. Corporation records from 1668 show that an ox, a wether (neutered ram) and a calf were ordered for the bishop's table at the castle.

Not long afterwards, however, the castle began to be leased to principal families of the town. In 1682 the Southwell family moved in. They would stay for five terms of twenty-one years, altogether a hundred and five years, and would be very influential in Wisbech.

Charles II acted quickly to lift the austerity of the previous regime. All over the country, theatres, racetracks and taverns were re-opened, shaking off the dust in an atmosphere that was almost party-like.

He made church attendance compulsory again. For all Charles' love of the high life, he was keen to reassert the authority of the Church of England after Cromwell's slighting of it. In 1662, he introduced twice daily prayers. Between the second of February and the first of November, early morning prayers were to be said at 6am. In the winter months, from the second of November to the first of February, they would begin later, at 10am.

A huge coat of arms was hung in St Peter and St Paul's in Wisbech, where it remains very much in evidence today. The wooden galleries on the north and south sides, one of which had been built for John Thurloe, were left in place. With the recent boost in church attendance, the extra seating was very useful.

By this time, St Peter's had a peal of eight bells. As was usual in England, the bells had been ringing the curfew for centuries. The curfew sounded every night at 9pm and morning bells rang out at 5am in summer, 6am in winter. Between the evening curfew and morning bells, the townspeople were expected to stay indoors and put out all fires and candles. This tradition had stemmed from the time of the monasteries. Keeping people off the streets at night was a good deterrent against lawlessness and extinguishing fires was just good sense. Even by the reign of Charles II, most buildings were still made of wood and thatch and easily caught fire.

Church bells had sounded across the English landscape since Saxon times. Crowland Abbey is believed to have been the first ecclesiastical building in England to have been equipped with bells, having boasted six of them since around AD 960. Steeples in which to hang the bells were gradually added to churches from that time on. A Passing Bell, to announce the death of a townsperson so that prayers could be said for the departing soul, had still been tolled in Wisbech until at least the end of the sixteenth century.

The Church was beginning to flex its new muscles and this was more apparent in some parishes than in others. In 1670, nine excommunications were handed out in Gedney, Lincolnshire. Two more followed in 1674 and sixteen in 1677.

On June the fifth 1687, John Garner and Robertson Thornton were elected as churchwardens for the parish of Gedney. At that time, if a parishioner was elected as churchwarden he was obliged to accept the role. These two men, however, refused to take the oath and serve. The Reverend Augustin Fish denounced them 'excommunicate' as a result. It would seem, though, that Robertson Thornton's objection was more against the priest than the role itself. When he was taken to Lincoln he took his oath to serve as a warden without any fuss and was then absolved of excommunication.

Two years later, two other Gedney parishioners found themselves in trouble. John Austin and James Waseldine were excommunicated by the Reverend Augustin Fish for their contumacy, in other words their cheek and stubbornness, and their refusal to pay church tithes.

It is hard to say whether these punishments were as common in other parishes and that records have simply been lost, or whether the Reverend Augustin Fish was just keen on handing out excommunications.

On a worldlier subject, in 1668 Charles II renewed Wisbech's charter. The annual elections of ten Capital Burgesses and the town bailiff still had to take place, but the new charter's instructions were more detailed than before.

All freeholders of the town with an annual income of forty shillings or more were still required to assemble in the common hall at midday on each November the second. The previous year's burgesses had also to be present, so that their service and conduct over the preceding twelve months could be publicly reviewed. The townspeople were invited to voice any opinions on the outgoing burgesses' performance. Depending on how well this went, a burgess could then stand for re-election, together with other suitable candidates, provided that they had attended Mass within the last year.

A returning officer and two clerks were appointed and a poll paper was written out. The meeting then adjourned to the grammar school next door where hustings, a temporary platform on which the candidates stood, had been set up. The poll remained open until midnight and each freeholder was allowed to vote for ten names on the list.

Because of the restrictions on the townspeople's eligibility to vote, the number of voters must have been modest, but even so election day was quite an event. Wine and cakes were laid on for the assembly, prompting quite a few gentlemen to hang around all day, drinking and becoming steadily more boisterous. The expense and public nuisance led to the cost being capped at six pounds, but even that bought enough wine to bring about disorder. In the end, the whole catering side of things was dropped.

At midnight, voting stopped and the votes were counted. The number of votes for each candidate was read out and the ten new Capital Burgesses were announced for the coming year. The new burgesses then decided amongst themselves who should take on the role of bailiff.

The duties of the burgesses no longer included the administration of local justice, their authority stretching only as far as the management of the corporate borough's estates. The revenue collected from these estates, together with the profit from fairs and markets, amounted to about £2000 a year, with which the town was run.

Still on the subject of finance, by 1670 there was a national shortage of coins. During the turbulence of recent times, insufficient coinage had been minted and the shortfall had to be made up somehow. Individual towns and even private individuals stepped in to create their own currency.

Halfpenny and farthing coins called tokens were minted from copper. In 1671 the Wisbech town bailiff spent £20 on producing halfpenny tokens. Most of them were inscribed with 'A Wisbech Half Penny' on one side and the town's arms on the reverse.

Around two hundred years later, when St Peter and St Paul's Church was undergoing repairs, a few small, thin copper coins were discovered lying on a long buried earlier floor of flat glazed tiles. These flooring tiles were an interesting find in themselves, being typical of old ecclesiastical buildings. At two and a half centimetres in thickness and ten centimetres square, the tiles were well decorated and made to last. The coins lying on them, though, were of even greater interest. They showed that members of Wisbech's trade guilds were producing their own tokens. One of them was inscribed 'Wisbitch H I' on one side and 'Henry Tunard', with the arms of the bakers' guild, on the other.

When the government caught up with coin production, tokens were recalled. They were collected and handed in to locally authorised tradesmen who took them to be exchanged for silver.

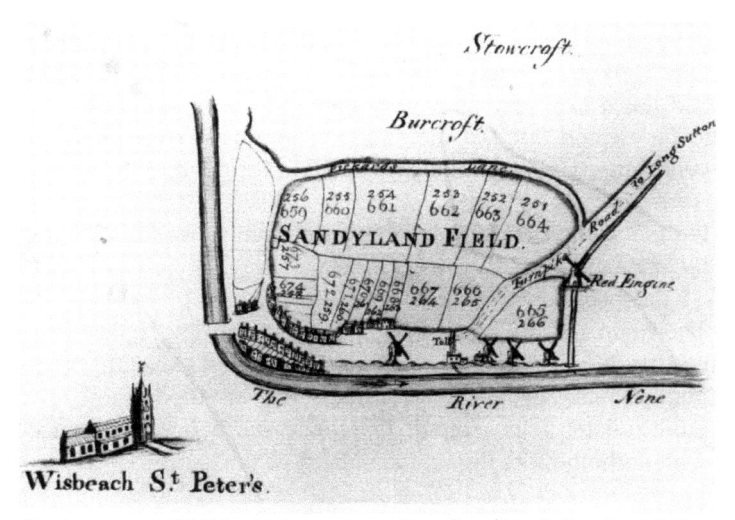

Later copy of 17th century map showing Sandyland and the Old Market (with permission of Wisbech and Fenland Museum)

However well Wisbech was run, its amenities were still basic. Town drainage was slightly improved by this time, in that some of the sewers ran underground. One of these drainage tunnels, which was repaired in 1677, ran north of Pickards Lane and drained water from the Old Market. Another ran the length of the main market place, but there were still a number of open sewers, such as the one along High Street which continued in front of the Horn and Pheasant (later the Rose and Crown).

Anything from rain water to butchery residue from the shambles found its way into the sewers, both the open and underground variety. From there, the waste was washed into the river. During dry periods, when there was insufficient water to flush the waste along the channels, rubbish of all sorts accumulated to rot. It must have created a terrible stink.

It would be a long time before the town's drainage systems became more sophisticated, but at least something was being done about the water supply. There had been a pond in the Old Market for many years and by 1669 its constant neglect had left it in a very unhealthy state. The burgesses ordered it to be cleared out and the situation improved even more ten years later when the pond was filled in for good.

On the second of March 1679 a new pump was installed in its place. This really was progress!

The main market place had already undergone a facelift. It had been resurfaced in 1665 and it is likely that the water pump which appears on later maps was installed at this time. Unfortunately, the square had once more been resurfaced with nothing more durable than hard-packed soil.

There were some attempts to save the townspeople's feet from the muddy streets, however. Planks were laid across the worst patches of mud and those used to cross High Street remained in use until the early 1800s. There were also posts for tethering horses at regular intervals along the street.

Pedestrians were further assisted by the introduction of three crossing places of flag stones over the open sewer. One of these crossing places was close to the front door of the Horn and Pheasant, at the end of the market place. This crossing was known as the Crying Stone, the place where the town crier stood to deliver official announcements to the townspeople.

Town criers were officers of the court, who since medieval times had made pronouncements to a largely illiterate populace. In Wisbech, the crier summoned his audience by ringing a hand bell and people gathered to hear what he had to say. Standing so close to the open sewer can't have been too pleasant, so with any hope the announcements were kept short.

Even in London, the streets had no pavements until 1673 and it would be a further sixty years before they came to Wisbech. Even then, they would be nothing more than a border of pebbles running close by the houses. In the meantime, everyone had to make do with planks.

Conditions were gradually improving for the town's prisoners. By 1682 the rent paid to Wisbech by the Isle of Ely for keeping a gaol had risen to £14 a year and the burgesses were doing their best to improve the prison's facilities. When the gaol yard wall was rebuilt to make an outside area for the inmates' use, they could at least benefit from a little fresh air.

The population of Wisbech in 1676 was 1,705. It was still modest in size, but the town certainly knew how to stand up for itself.

Its trade was flourishing. Though the port was by then two miles inland, coal, fish, salt and all sorts of other goods were coming in by river. With all this trade came wealth, but there was a snag. The Port of King's Lynn, having grown steadily in importance since the rerouting of the River Ouse in the thirteenth century, held jurisdiction over the Port of Wisbech.

King's Lynn therefore dictated how the Port of Wisbech should operate. During the 1670s Lynn customs officers issued a mandate stipulating where vessels were permitted to tie up and unload on the Wisbech quayside. Seeing these orders as unreasonable, Wisbech's port officials refused to comply, continuing to allow ships to dock wherever practical. The Corporation of Lynn was not happy and brought a suit against the Capital Burgesses of Wisbech in his majesty's exchequer.

On the sixteenth of October 1676 four commissioners were sent to survey the Port of Wisbech. They concluded that the wharf from the Bull Stairs (near New Inn Yard) to the far corner of Ship Lane, which measured about a hundred and sixteen metres in length, should be designated for the loading, discharging and shipping of all goods, wares and merchandise in the port.

But better news was to follow. The absolute independence of the Port of Wisbech was declared in 1680.

To celebrate, the Capital Burgesses set about improving the port. First of all, they applied to the Trinity House of Deptford Stroud for powers of beaconage. This allowed them to place buoys and beacons in the approach channel for the safety of ships heading for the port. Having done this, they were entitled to charge ship masters for coming into port and this income helped to defray their costs. By May 1710, a curator was appointed to look after the new buoys and beacons. He also collected his majesty's customs, subtracted the town's beaconage fees and presented his accounts to the bailiff.

Yet despite this progress, the condition of the river between Wisbech and the sea had been allowed to deteriorate. The constant build-up of silt in the river was hampering navigation to such an extent that no vessel of more than thirty tons could reach the port. This was hardly helpful to trade, but nothing would be done about it for quite some time.

Meanwhile, people living on the open Fen were learning to adapt to a different way of life. Not everywhere had been drained though; the meres of Ramsey, Ugg and Whittlesey had been left largely unaffected, but other areas had been successfully turned over to agriculture. Some landowners were even receiving income from their newly drained acres. One example of this was on land near Morton's Leam which had been enclosed around 1664. Tithes there were at last being paid to the Church, as landowner, in respect of the first wheat harvests.

But things were rarely straight forward. In 1675, coleseed, later to be known as rape, was grown for the first time in the parish of St Peter and St Paul in Wisbech. It produced a good harvest, but because there was no ruling on the payment of tithes on this previously unknown crop, a dispute broke out. The vicar demanded his tithe and his coleseed growing parishioners refused. Even prosperity brings its share of problems, it seems.

Other agricultural news was a lot more serious. Despite the new drainage channels and high banks, fields in many areas were not draining well. Floods were still occurring and crops were still failing.

It wasn't long before the cause of this new problem became obvious. The peat was shrinking.

Much of the newly drained land was peat fen, of which ninety-five percent was water. When peat is allowed to dry out, it quickly shrinks. Ever since the major drainage works of the 1650s, the level of the peat had gradually been falling, by about two and a half centimetres a year. Unnoticed at first, with every passing year the shrinkage had become more evident. Now, thirty years or so since the completion of work, the problem was clear to see. In many places, the fields had dropped so much that they were lower than the rivers.

The drainage system relied on fields being at a higher level than the rivers, so that water could drain easily from the higher land into the lower water channels. However, with the peat fields shrinking to below the level of the rivers, this gravity fed drainage was no longer possible.

Even the outflow of rivers into the sea was affected. Where the lower peat Fen met the higher level of silt at the edge of the Wash, the flow of water out to sea was severely hampered.

And there was another problem; the Fen Blow. This occurred when the peat dried out so much that its surface was reduced to fine powder. In high winds this fine top soil was easily blown from the fields, creating dense, black clouds of dust which found their way into every home in their path. Dust even managed to get into clothes and bedding. Even more importantly, as the soil blew from the fields in spring, it took the season's newly planted seeds with it.

Vermuyden had not foreseen the problems caused by peat shrinkage. It was an alarming setback and a solution was urgently needed.

It was windmills which came to the rescue, at least for some of the problems. These wind engines had been used here and there since the 1580s, but were still unpopular with Fenmen, who distrusted the new-fangled 'gewgaws'.

Despite their lack of popularity, they were the answer to many prayers. By the end of the 1670s many new wind engines had been installed. They could raise water by as much as one and a half metres and discharge it into a higher level drain. Made from timber, the mills were around twelve metres tall with a moveable cap. Attached to this cap were canvas covered sails. Each mill was equipped with a water wheel of about seven metres in diameter, fitted with attachments to scoop up water.

Men were hired to live part of the year in the mill and look after it. It was a full time job. The keeper moved into the mill in September and remained there throughout the winter. From early morning until late at night he had to be on hand to work the chain and windlass which manoeuvred the engine's upper section to present the sails to the wind. This ability to turn the sails according to the wind direction was useful, but the sails were not strong enough to tolerate high winds. When gales threatened, the keeper had to climb up the sails and gather in the canvas to prevent it tearing. Health and safety were not the greatest concerns in those days!

The keeper stayed at the mill until April or May, when summer conditions generally brought a reduced risk of high water. He moved into a nearby cottage to spend the summer maintaining ditches.

However hard the mills and their keepers worked, the problems were not solved immediately. Most of the windmills were privately owned, positioned to keep the owner's land dry, and there was no coordination between the individual mills. Often, excess water lifted from an area ended up in ditches which were too full or blocked to contain it. This inevitably led to damaged banks and new outbreaks of flooding.

In the end, the Bedford Level Commission had to step in and control the positioning of new mills. They refused permission for some and even demolished badly placed existing ones.

In the new post-drainage era, therefore, things were still far from perfect. Despite decades of ingenuity and hard labour, flooding still occurred. The 'Dry Land' wasn't doing a lot of 'smiling'.

Many new landowners found farming very challenging. Floods, which were no longer supposed to happen, frequently destroyed their crops. When high water levels in the ditches warned of imminent floods, church bells were tolled, sounding their alarm across the fields to warn the farmers. This gave them time to gather their livestock and flee to the 'islands' of higher ground, but nothing could be done to save their crops. In some cases, their losses were so bad that the newcomers gave up altogether and left the area.

Few Fen Tigers, as they stood their ground and withstood the hardships of another winter, would have spared the 'foreigners' much sympathy.

Some years later, in the early 1700s, the novelist and diarist Daniel Defoe visited the Fens and described land still covered in water and heavy fog. He wrote that when the higher ground was 'gilded with sun', the Isle of Ely appeared 'as if wrapped up in blankets.'

Some newcomers, however, had managed to brave the harsh conditions and had settled in. These were the descendants of the Scottish and Dutch prisoners of war who had survived their toil on the banks and drains in the 1650s. Having endured years of hard labour, they perhaps found everyday Fenland life a pleasant respite, and sent for their families to join them.

Though they are rarely mentioned, the Fens also experienced dry periods and hot summers. Thomas Baskerville, a diarist who toured England in 1681, visited the Fens during one hot early summer.

His description of Ely was far from complimentary. In the May of 1681, he and his party entered Ely on horseback from the Fen along the river. The English spring had been scorching with too little rain, according to Master Baskerville, and had followed a dry winter. Together with the 'effects of the late comet', as he put it, it had dried out the land terribly. Many of the bridges he used to cross ditches and streams had rotted. He hardly dared to cross some of them on horseback for fear that the horses might fall through, into the 'rotten bogs' below. He described evil smelling vapours emanating from the ditches in the suffocating May heat. He and his companions could hardly breathe as they rode along, noting 'poor cottages and wretched farms.' He did add, though, that there were plenty of red shanks and other birds for the Fen people to hunt.

His mood hardly improved on entering Ely itself. 'The buildings of the town are very indifferent,' he wrote, but finally saw something to lift his spirits. He added, 'the structure of the cathedral...is very noble and stately to look on.'

Charles II coat of arms in St Peter's Church (with permission of the parish church)

Refuge in Wisbech

King Charles II, though he had many illegitimate children, died in 1685 without leaving an heir. He was succeeded by his brother, James, the Duke of York.

King James II did not reign for long. His Catholicism awakened memories of past religious turmoil and the fear that more could come. His popularity diminished even further when he tried to create religious liberty for English Catholics and Protestant non-conformists. His sense of what was right was seriously at odds with that of the Church of England.

The Fens, though not greatly affected by the king's religious leanings, witnessed the results of religious strife elsewhere.

Many Huguenots (French Protestants) arrived in England in 1685, having escaped persecution in their Catholic homeland. Smaller groups of Huguenots had arrived earlier in the century, as feeling against them grew in France. In 1685 all hope of them being able to remain in their own country died when their civil rights were officially cancelled.

Many of the refugees were artisans; skilled weavers, joiners and smiths. They settled wherever there was work and many thousands went to east London, where they became established in crafts such as silk weaving and as silversmiths.

Groups of Huguenots came to live in the Fens. Some settled in Thorney and others found work in Parson Drove. Like the Dutch and Scottish before them, the French became integrated, their culture blending with that of Fenland.

There was another refugee who arrived in the Fens at around this time, one who is remembered affectionately as Wisbech's Princess.

Jane Stuart arrived in Wisbech at a time when life at court was falling apart. Her father, King James II, had fallen even more out of favour with his subjects and the rifts created by the religious changes he wanted to introduce resulted in 'the glorious revolution' of 1688.

This was a very grand title for what really happened. Frustrated by the king and his Catholic ideas, leading nobles invited the king's Protestant son-in-law, William of Orange, to come to England and talk sense into James. Rather than talk, however, William took the crown for himself.

When he landed in England with more troops than was strictly necessary for a chat, James fled the country. His leaving was interpreted as abdication.

In the midst of this turmoil, Jane, who was one of James' many illegitimate children, left the court in London and made her slow way north. She had become a Quaker during her time at court and sought a simple, anonymous life, far away from the intrigues of London. She found her way to Wisbech and soon found help and friendship in the Quaker community there. (Quakers were also known as 'Friends'.)

By this time, Jane was about thirty-four years of age. She worked on the land as a reaper to start with, setting up home in the cellar of a house in the Old Market. The house was later rebuilt and is now 'Granny's Cupboard Antiques', but the cellar remains much as it was in Jane's day. Her accommodation, consisting of a few, dark rooms and an open fire, would have been basic but no worse than most ordinary homes of the time.

She soon found new work spinning worsted on a wheel at home. She sold her yarn on the market and it is thought to have been while working there that she caught sight of a coach bearing the arms of the Duke of Argyle outside the Horn and Pheasant. Anxious not to be discovered, she packed up her stock and ran home.

The throne had passed to William of Orange and his wife Mary, the daughter of King James. Though crowned jointly as William III and Mary II to strengthen their claim to the throne, there was always the risk that other contenders might try to take it from them. Before James II had gone into exile, his queen, Mary of Modena, had given birth to a son, also called James. There had been a rumour, however, that the baby wasn't their son at all, but had been smuggled into the palace in a warming pan. King William was keen to encourage these rumours. If true, they would mean that the young James had no claim to the throne.

The new king's men went in search of any witnesses who might have been able to support the warming pan story. As one of James' illegitimate children, Jane would have been at the centre of court life. Her father was known to have treated all of his children with great affection and it is likely that Jane and her siblings were present at the birth. The Duke of Argyle, as one of the king's men, must have been keen to speak to her, therefore. Jane, however, wanted nothing more to do with the world she had left behind and remained undiscovered, living quietly in Wisbech with her Quaker friends.

Life was made a little easier for Quakers and other non-conformists by the Toleration Act of 1689. The Act granted increased freedom of worship, meaning that Quakers needed no longer to hold their meetings secretly in private houses or secluded orchards. In 1711 they established their first Meeting House in Wisbech, converting two thatched cottages by the river. A later, Victorian, Meeting House still occupies the same position on North Brink, next door to buildings belonging to Peckover House. Jane Stuart's grave can still be seen in the small yard behind the Meeting House.

Jane's half-sister, Mary II ruled with her husband William until her death from smallpox in 1694. William then ruled alone until his death in 1702.

Despite increased religious tolerance, the end of the seventeenth century was a difficult time for the English. A shortage of grain led to inflated prices and hunger. The Fens, with their continuing drainage problems, still could not produce enough wheat to meet demand. Extra supplies of wheat, rye and malt had to be brought in by river from Suffolk, but it was a slow process due to the condition of the waterways.

In 1699, the Capital Burgesses of Wisbech, together with Justices of the Peace, deputy lieutenants and other freeholders of Newton, Leverington, Tydd St Giles, Elm, Upwell, Outwell, Guyhirn, Parson Drove and Murrow decided to take action. They signed a petition requesting that the River Lark be made navigable. This was a tributary of the Ouse which crossed the border between Suffolk and Cambridgeshire and its improvement would have made the import of grain a lot easier.

In the meantime, there were more problems to cope with than mere delivery delays. Even when the grain eventually reached the Fens, it was too expensive for the poorest people. Increased hunger led to riots which were mercilessly punished. At the Wisbech Assizes of 1703 fourteen people were found guilty of rioting. Court records noted rather coldly that not *all* of them were executed.

For people at the other end of the income scale, there was tax to pay. There had nearly always been tax of some kind, of course, but now the rules were changing. As far back as the Magna Carta of 1215, a fifteenth part of the value of a person's moveable goods had had to be paid to the king. Later, this had increased to three fifteenths. When it still hadn't been enough to keep the royal coffers full, a subsidy had been added. By the early years of Queen Elizabeth's reign, the national subsidy had totalled £120,000.

During the reign of William and Mary, these payments were standardised and referred to as land tax. More precisely, the mandate was 'an Act for granting their Majesties an aid of four shillings in the pound for one year of carrying on a vigorous war against France.'

Despite taxation, life for the privileged classes could be very enjoyable. A few wealthy, adventurous individuals were taking lengthy breaks away from home, setting out on foreign tours and trips across Britain. Many of these intrepid travellers, such as Thomas Baskerville mentioned earlier, wrote down their observations and impressions in journals.

These personal views provide a valuable insight into life as it once was. The only glimpses of earlier times had been through court and church records, which were rarely generous with detail. The later diarists, however, who probably never expected anyone to read their scribbling, gave their opinions freely.

One such explorer was the granddaughter of Lord Saye and Sele, an independent and imperious lady who travelled through regions of England accompanied by only one maidservant. She gave her memoirs the lengthy title of 'Through England on a Side Saddle in the Time of William and Mary, being the Diary of Celia Fiennes.'

In 1698 she described Ely as 'the dirtiest place I ever saw', unconsciously agreeing with Thomas Baskerville's earlier comments. She went on to give her opinion of the local people, whom she called 'Fen Slodgers', as 'a lazy sort of people.'

Celia also wrote about her visit to Whittlesey Mere, explaining that it was, 'part of the ffenny country'. Whittlesey Mere, unmolested so far by drainage schemes, was still a great body of water. It had an abundance of fish and at its centre was a small island which was a good breeding ground for wildfowl.

Celia noted that the mere was difficult to reach because of the marshy land surrounding it. There were, however, channels running into it, so that the open water could be reached by boat. Celia must have visited during unsettled weather, because she described how the wind could 'rise like hurricanes' when the water looked formidable and dangerous.

But despite its stormy and treacherous darker side, Whittlesey Mere was enjoyed by many over the centuries.

In 1669 a water party had been held there at which Mr William Pierrepont, the brother of the Marquess of Dorchester, entertained the bishop and other clergy of Peterborough Cathedral. They had eaten melons served with sugar, salt or pepper, according to taste, and port wine. Then there had been venison pasties, beef, mutton, poultry and more wine. They had finished their meal with roasted apples, tarts, cakes, cider and even more wine. After all this rather fine dining, the host had lit a bonfire and his guests smoked tobacco from a silver box.

It wasn't just the elite who enjoyed days by the mere. Regattas and water picnics were held there regularly, drawing in folk from all around to enjoy music and buy refreshments from the booths set up around the lake.

The mere was often described as a beautiful place with an attractive shoreline and jetties. Many species of wild flower and fern grew there and it was home to many species of butterfly. Nineteenth century drainage would eventually see an end to all of it, but for the foreseeable future people would be able to enjoy the mere's benefits. It would also continue to provide a living for the people who fished its waters and kept its swans.

Fortunately for Whittlesey folk, when it came to new drainage schemes, attention was consistently focused elsewhere. In 1713, the sluice at Denver collapsed. That particular stretch of the Ouse had been in a bad way for some time, its outfall choked with silt and its river banks eroded. The surrounding area was almost permanently under water and ships had given up trying to navigate along its course.

Now without a sluice, and with river traffic ground to a halt, local people returned for a time to old ways. Punts and other small boats were brought back into use for wildfowling and fishing. While the people of Denver smiled at their unexpected good fortune, the authorities scratched their heads about how and when the sluice could be rebuilt. It would be another forty years before it was.

Meanwhile, the country had acquired a new monarch and England had gained new status.

William and Mary had died without an heir and so Mary's sister Anne had become queen in 1702. She inherited the crowns of England (which encompassed Wales and Ireland) and Scotland. However, under the Acts of Union of 1706 and 07, England and Scotland were united as a single sovereign state called Great Britain.

Whether or not it was to celebrate the new union, in 1711 St Peter and St Paul's Church obtained its first organ. It was installed at the western end of the church by C Quarles of Cambridge. It was still far from common for churches to have an organ at that time and its early installation is an indication of the town's prosperity.

The Stuart dynasty came to an end with the death of Queen Anne in 1714. She too died childless and so it was the Hanoverian King George I who succeeded her to the throne. He introduced a whole new era, one of significant change and development for the country and a time of increasing prosperity for Wisbech.

Great Britain's new colonies in North America, the Caribbean and India were bringing in huge wealth. Until the 1650s, the great majority of the national export had been wool. Now, however, goods such as sugar, tobacco and Indian calico from the colonies made up around thirty percent of British export. Wool was reduced to forty-seven percent.

In an attempt to bolster the wool trade, the Burial in Wool Acts were introduced in 1667 and 68. Under the new ruling, burial shrouds had to be made of wool. A relative of the deceased had to swear within eight days of the burial that wool had been used for the shroud, incurring a fine of five pounds for using any other material.

Poised on the threshold of the Georgian age, Wisbech had a lot to be cheerful about. A petition to the House of Commons in 1719 supplied plentiful information in support of its request that no more salt marsh be embanked in order to preserve the true nature of the marsh. (It sounds almost modern!) The petition tells us a lot about the port at that time.

As an ancient sea port, the petition explained, Wisbech had more than thirty ships regularly importing wine, iron, deals (softwood), coal, potash, pitch, tar, hemp and other commodities. This trade produced an annual income to his majesty of £4,000. Annual exports included a thousand tons of linseed oil and forty thousand quarts of oats. As well as the larger ships, there were around thirty smaller vessels of twenty or thirty tons used for unloading the larger vessels and carrying goods to and from neighbouring ports.

The port provided employment for a large number of seafaring men and quayside workers, greatly benefitting the region. Between Christmas 1718 and Christmas 1719, two hundred and forty-one ships or more were said to have cleared the port.

So much coming and going meant plenty of business for the town's hostelries. The old Horn and Pheasant in the New Market had at some point changed its name to the Rose and Crown. It had also been extended during the last century to accommodate its increased trade, stable blocks being added with guest rooms upstairs. Guests could now sleep in rooms above where their horse was stabled, reaching their accommodation via an open balcony. Some of these balconies can still be seen at the back of the hotel.

Sadly, not every visitor was impressed with the town. In another entry from Daniel Defoe's diary of the early 1700s he said about Wisbech that there was 'nothing that way to tempt our curiosity but deep roads, innumerable drains and dykes of water, all navigable, and a rich soil, the land bearing a vast quantity of good hemp, but a base unwholesome air.'

But on the whole, things were looking good for Wisbech. There would always be difficulties, of course. Bad winters, poor summers and grain shortages would all take their toll, but there would also be cause for optimism.

Linseed oil would continue as a major export for a long time to come. The flax seed grown to produce it would thrive on the newly drained and fertile land and by 1735 there would be at least seven mills in Wisbech used for the production of this valuable export. One would be in the Old Market and another on the site of the present Elgood's Brewery. The location of the others is yet to be determined!

Despite the dashed hopes and loss of the traditional way of life of many Fen people, East Anglia would by 1750 become the most important source of grain for the London market.

Wisbech and the Fens were more than ready for the Georgian age.

CHAPTER EIGHT

Doublets and Chamber Pots; The Way They Lived

Having traced the progress of Wisbech and the Fens from the end of the medieval age to the coming of the Georgians, it seems a good idea to look at how the people of those times lived.

It is time, then, to take a quick peep into their world.

From Shutter to Sash; Where They Lived

For centuries, English buildings had been constructed with stone, wattle and daub. Stone for Fenland churches, monasteries and other principal buildings had been transported on lighters along the waterways from the quarry at Barnack, near Peterborough. Materials such as timber, mud and straw for simpler buildings, meanwhile, were more locally sourced.

But then, during the late 1400s arrived the house brick. Enormously expensive at first, and used only for the finest buildings, bricks gradually became more affordable and were more widely used.

What really transformed the English landscape, though, was the dissolution of the monasteries of the 1530s. As Henry VIII seized Church land and sold it to new owners, the distribution of English wealth was changed forever. Whereas once the largest and most powerful landowner after the king had been the Church, its land was now spread amongst a multitude of private owners.

Ancient abbey buildings, even if not already left in ruins by Thomas Cromwell's men, were usually demolished by their new owners. The dressed stone was then sold for reuse elsewhere. In a few cases though, parts of the buildings survived and were incorporated into new residences.

Many thousands of people who had rented their homes from the monasteries now found themselves with new landlords. Whether this was a change for the better or worse depended, of course, on the local situation, but in some areas the new owners reinvested their profits into the renovation or rebuilding of their tenants' homes.

In most cases, such improvements were long overdue. Some of the poorest dwellings, often no more than single roomed huts, had not been repaired or improved for decades. In these homes, life went on around a central hearth fire, the smoke finding its way through the thatched roof without the aid of a chimney. A layer of smoke tended to form a few feet above the ground, making it more comfortable to sleep on the floor, below the smoke line.

Straw or rushes were usually strewn over the floor of hard packed earth, though more sophisticated flooring could be created by plaiting reeds or rushes into mats. Going to bed normally meant nestling down in the straw, though more comfort could be achieved by filling a hessian sack with bedding straw to make a basic mattress. Fenlanders were perhaps more fortunate in this respect, many of them sleeping on mattresses stuffed with goose feathers, from the wild birds they caught.

Windows, if they existed at all, were simple openings protected by rough wooden shutters. Any 'glazing' consisted of thin sheets of parchment or horn. There was little or no furniture. Meals were eaten on boards supported by trestles which were packed away at night to make sleeping space. The lavatory was usually an earth pit in the yard which had to be re-dug periodically.

Depending on the availability of local materials, old half timbered and thatched cottages were rebuilt by the new landowners in stone or brick. Many of the new homes had tiled roofs. A chimney with a stone fireplace against one wall replaced the old central hearth, and some homes even had a second storey. This was generally reached by a short flight of stairs supported by a central newel post. These were real improvements for folk used to smoky, cramped living conditions.

Towards the opposite end of the housing scale, some of the old manor houses retained their central hearth arrangement for longer, but by the 1570s even these were having chimneys installed with large, stone, decorative fireplaces.

The fashionable Tudor homes of the wealthy had carved wooden panelling in the principal rooms. Their plastered ceilings were decorated with elaborate mouldings of fruit and flowers and any unpanelled walls were covered with tapestries. Together with heavy, carved oak furniture and plump cushions, they gave these homes a warm, luxurious feel.

Unlike the poor, a wealthy family would have had at least one 'proper' bed, as we would think of it now. The master and mistress of the house would have a bed complete with curtains, covers and mattresses, while other family members might sleep in a truckle bed which was wheeled under the main one when not in use. Servants slept on the floor.

For the leisured classes with the inclination to create gardens around their homes, parterres had become fashionable. These were created by planting tiny box hedges in elaborate patterns and filling the beds between with sweet smelling flowers and herbs.

Until well into Queen Elizabeth's reign, English townscapes were still late medieval in appearance. Streets were lined with half timbered buildings, their upper storeys projecting slightly over the lower ones. By the 1580s, however, flatter fronted buildings had become desirable and in some towns whole streets were refaced with brick. Attic rooms, lit by dormer windows, were also added to some buildings.

A shop or workshop which fronted on to the street usually took up the whole ground floor of these townhouses, with reception rooms arranged on the upper floors. Daily life was gradually moving away from the old multi-use of communal rooms and it was becoming fashionable to have a room dedicated to dining. These new dining rooms were well but simply furnished with oak chairs, tables and pewter candlesticks. Kitchens were often housed in the back extensions added to townhouses at this time.

Even in the countryside, the style of houses was changing. For centuries, the homes of the well-to-do had been arranged around a central hall, open to the rafters and usually two storeys high. These halls were gradually being replaced by single storey versions with flat, plastered ceilings. They were no longer used as communal rooms in which the whole household ate and the servants slept. They were now more likely to be used for the reception of guests, though servants probably still ate there, leaving the dining room solely for the family's use.

Window glass had always been an expensive luxury, as it had had to be imported. Bess of Hardwick, the Countess of Shrewsbury, was well known for her extravagant use of glass in her Derbyshire mansion. The windows of

Hardwick Hall were so numerous and large that the walls appeared to be made purely of glass.

By the 1590s, however, glass production had begun in England, removing import costs and making it less expensive. As a result, even the middle classes could afford glass. Large bay windows consisting of many small panes became fashionable, but they were not popular for long. As handsome as they were, these huge expanses of glass made rooms far too hot in summer and too cold in winter. Few of them were equipped with shutters, and curtains failed to keep out the cold. By 1620, windows had become smaller again.

Another significant development in building design was in the stairs. Before the 1580s, all staircases had either been straight uncomplicated flights, or were spiralled around a newel post. By the early 1600s, however, wooden stairs could be cantilevered out from the wall, removing the need for a central support and giving hallways an open, airy feel.

The homes of successful members of the lower classes also benefitted from improvements. This was particularly true of the yeomen farmers. Usually quite well educated, they owned their land and employed local people, but also did some of the heavy work themselves. Their homes tended to be built from local materials and were generally only one room deep. Normally three or four rooms wide, they had upper floors and at least one chimney stack. They were simply furnished, typically with a table, benches, a bed, linen and one or two coffers.

Below the yeomen farmers on the social scale were the husbandmen who rented their land and were less well educated. Below them were the cottagers and labourers who made up a quarter of the population. Usually without any education at all, they worked as servants and relied on the goodness of their landlord for the condition of the homes they rented.

However much the design of Tudor homes changed, there was little improvement in sanitation. Where there was no cesspit, chamber pots and other waste continued to be thrown into the nearest drain or river.

Thorpe Hall in Longthorpe, Peterborough

The civil war, of course, was a time of destruction, rather than construction. Castles which had dominated the landscape since the twelfth century were systematically blown up or knocked down to punish their royalist owners and to wipe out symbols of the old social order. Even in Wisbech, the castle was dismantled during the Protectorate and the plot sold off. Many aristocratic families abandoned all hope of repairing their once stately homes and moved into new, more conveniently designed mansions.

Fighting, siege and occupation during the war years caused significant damage to many English towns and villages. The suppressed years of the Protectorate which followed saw the rebuilding of some of these places, but in a style much plainer than before.

Larger buildings were constructed in a handsome but unembellished way. The dominant feature of these houses was the hipped roof without gables, all four sides sloping down to meet the wall tops. These buildings were generally at least two rooms deep, which gave them a squarer floor plan. Their windows and doors were topped by plain triangular or semi-circular pediments. Thorpe Hall in Peterborough, built for Cromwell's Lord Chief Justice, Oliver St John, and Thurloe's Mansion, which graced the heart of Wisbech, are two examples of homes built in this style.

Architects, as we think of them today, came into being at around this time. Before then, buildings had been designed and built by master craftsmen, but now designers from gentlemanly origins were becoming prominent. One of these gentlemen, Inigo Jones, had earlier in the century designed the magnificent Queen's House for Anne of Denmark, the queen of James I. Later designers, such as Henry Bell, Sir Christopher Wren and Sir John Vanbrugh, were of similar origins and worked much as modern architects do. They still, however, worked closely with master craftsmen.

With the restoration of the monarchy in 1660 came a great outpouring of ideas and creativity. This new, bright era stimulated an increase in painting, sculpture, music, literature and architecture, all of which was of great interest to Charles II.

But then, in 1666, came the Great Fire of London. It was catastrophic. The old City, which had hardly changed from its medieval layout of timber buildings, was completely annihilated. Fire spread through it with appalling ease, destroying thirteen thousand houses, eighty-seven parish churches, and the mighty St Paul's Cathedral. The loss of life, devastation and homelessness caused by the fire would take years to overcome.

Where once there had been the old City of London, there was nothing but a barren space. It all had to be reconstructed from scratch and a huge programme of rebuilding began, incorporating wider streets and new, stricter building regulations. The Act for the Rebuilding of London of 1667 required all new buildings to be of stone or brick. Wood was only to be used for the beams over doors and windows. Further Acts of 1707 and 1709 added extra regulations, which led not only to increased fire resistance in buildings all over the country, but also to a new wave of design.

London, by the beginning of the eighteenth century, had a completely new look, its wide streets lined with neat, flat fronted houses. Most still had a shop, workshop or office on the ground floor, a basement and a yard at the back. Rooms were arranged symmetrically around a central staircase hall, with a dining room on the first floor and one or two floors of bedrooms above, plus a garret in the roof space. Altogether, it was usual for these houses to have between five and eight rooms.

There was now more space for the family and servants. Servants were an essential part of middle class life, both for status and practicality. Most were female domestics who worked in the basement kitchen and slept in the garret, but larger households also employed male clerks and took on apprentices. Because all but the largest homes had only one staircase, employers and servants had no choice but to live closely together.

The rebuilding of the City had been well organised, a ready supply of materials coming in from the brick pits and kilns around London. Some items were even prefabricated. Though it seems such a modern convenience, windows, doors and cornices were already being manufactured to standard sizes from softwood (deal). The widespread use of softwood, such as pine, was new in itself. Before the fire, oak had been the most common timber used in building, but pine was easily imported from the Baltic and was plentiful. Wisbech's busy Timber Market was evidence of that.

It was new window design, though, which really changed the look of buildings of all classes. In around 1670, sash windows were introduced, replacing traditional casements. Casement windows had been set into stone, brick or timber transoms and mullions, the glass panes held in place with lead and supported by thin iron bars. Usually diamond shaped, the panes had always been very small, mostly due to cost.

Sash windows were completely different. Tall in appearance, they consisted of two vertically sliding frames, each having a number of rectangular glass panes between wooden glazing bars. A system of brass pulleys, cords and lead counterweights allowed the frames to slide, opening and closing the window. The size of panes gradually increased and the glazing bars became finer, reducing the weight and allowing more light into the room.

These tall windows, arranged symmetrically across the front of a building, became a key feature of architectural design from the late 1600s. Rows of handsome new homes appeared all over London and the West End, the area many wealthy householders had moved to after the fire.

Another feature of King Charles' new London was the town square. Attractive open spaces, such as the piazza in Covent Garden (now largely roofed over) and St James' Square, gave the city a spacious elegance.

Furniture was evolving too, with upholstery making an appearance for the first time. Before then, the only padding used in seating had been in the cushions placed on hard oak chairs, but now padding was incorporated into the seat itself. The first sofas were seen in around 1700 and, suitably inspired, wealthy householders furnished their best rooms with curtains, upholstery and bed covers in matching damask and velvet. Walnut replaced oak as the choice for fashionable furniture, and walls were decorated with paintings, rather than the tapestries of earlier times. Silver stayed as popular as ever, fashioned into wall sconces, mirrors, chandeliers, candlesticks and wine coolers.

However refined though, furniture was still only of secondary importance to the rooms themselves. Interior decoration had reached new heights. Walls were painted in delicate shades and smooth ceilings with elaborate plaster cornices made rooms look good, even when empty.

The new century also saw changes in the organisation of households. Larger homes were being designed with back stairs, meaning that servants could move around to do their work without bumping into their employers. Servants were becoming less visible, no longer eating in the hall, but in their own basement dining room.

The gardens of the rich were developing almost as rapidly as their homes. Sweeping lawns, statues, even bowling greens, replaced the formality of parterres. William and Mary's new garden at Hampton Court was designed to imitate a romanticised English landscape. The king and queen had a taste for the exotic too, collecting rare plants from as far away as the East Indies. They had glasshouses in which to propagate these rare specimens, as well as two orangeries.

Wisbech was not immune to all this development. In the town and along the river banks a mixture of styles would have been seen. Some buildings, such as King's Hall in Barton, were reminders of Elizabethan splendour, while others had the sleeker look of the late 1600s.

In 1722 the townhouse known today as Peckover House would be built. It was to be a showpiece for the latest design and building methods and would herald the Georgian era with all its architectural beauty.

But the town's inhabitants, whether rich or poor, needed occasionally to travel. So how did they manage to get about? What was life like on the open road?

Sliding sash window at the National Trust's Peckover House (with permission of the National Trust)

Headroom for Big Wigs: Travel

The roads of Tudor England were dreadful. Most of them were no more than muddy tracks which, even when resurfaced, were covered with nothing more substantial than a layer of earth. They became so churned up in winter that they were impassable to wheeled traffic for months at a time. The general absence of signposts meant that anyone travelling through unfamiliar territory relied on directions from strangers or the help of a guide.

Until the final years of Queen Elizabeth's reign, transport was as simple as it was slow. The wealthy rode on horseback and could travel between thirty-five and forty miles a day on a good horse. The infirm were carried on a litter. This was a chair or bed supported on poles and carried on the shoulders of between two and four people.

The poor generally walked everywhere, managing about three miles an hour, but mules, carts and wagons were used where available.

Carriages began to make an appearance in England towards the end of the 1500s. At first, they were lumbering, uncomfortable vehicles with no suspension to absorb the jarring of wheels over rough road surfaces and pot holes. Even so, they were expensive luxuries available only to the rich. A simple method of suspension was later invented in which the coach body was supported by leather straps. This cushioned the passengers from some of the jarring, but created a swaying motion instead, bad for anyone prone to travel sickness.

Early carriages had a door on each side and could seat four people in two pairs. The coachman driving the four horses sat on a high seat above the front wheels. At first, the windows were unglazed, covered only by blinds, which gave passengers very little protection from the elements. Window glass at last began to be fitted around 1680.

The introduction of these new four wheeled vehicles opened the door, so to speak, to public transport.

The stage coach made its appearance in England during the early 1600s. It carried passengers in stages of ten to fifteen miles, stopping at designated inns along the way so that the horses could be changed. Up to eight passengers, who paid the highest fare, could ride inside the coach itself. Second class passengers sat in a section attached to the back, but the cheapest seats were on the roof. These third class passengers had only a hand rail to save them from falling off and shared the roof with the luggage.

Stage coaches, being so heavily loaded, were not known for their speed, their teams of four to six horses managing only about four miles an hour. As with all wheeled transport, travelling by coach was slower than on horseback, but it enabled passengers to take luggage on long journeys. Coach travel wouldn't really speed up until the new designs of the early eighteenth century were introduced.

The first stage coach route was established between Edinburgh and Leith in 1610. Other routes followed and by the end of the 1600s a limited timetable of regular routes was in place. Travelling from London to Liverpool took ten days in summer, when the roads were at their best. London to Exeter and London to York were other well travelled roads.

Travellers relied heavily on the many coaching inns along the way. Unfortunately, most of them were as terrible as they were expensive. They quickly gained a reputation for being flea infested, overcrowded and for serving poor food. It was quite usual for guests to have to share rooms, even beds, with strangers.

London Hackney carriages were first available for hire by the end of the sixteenth century. In the beginning, they were mostly old family carriages sold off by the wealthy, but they gradually improved. It wasn't until 1634 though, that the first rank of Hackney carriages appeared in the Strand. Driven by liveried coachmen, they were an expensive way to travel.

Sedan chairs were somewhat cheaper to hire, but could only carry two passengers. They had evolved from an open litter into a tall enclosed cabin mounted on two horizontal poles and carried by two strong men. Although they first appeared in England in the early 1600s, they didn't really catch on until the 1630s.

Wealthy citizens soon acquired sedan chairs of their own, keeping them, without the poles, in the halls of their grand homes. They were extremely convenient for short distances and their height provided plenty of headroom for the big wigs which became fashionable later in the century. Passengers could be carried from their own hall, across town and up the front steps of the house they were visiting. They could then alight gracefully in their host's hall.

For the independent traveller, the maps of John Ogilby were a significant breakthrough. The strip maps he had published in the late 1670s showed the major routes across England, Scotland and Wales, together with useful landmarks. With the use of these maps, journeys could be more easily planned and even unfamiliar territory could be crossed without the need for a guide.

And having arrived at their destination, travellers needed to be fed. This seems a good opportunity, then, to look at what the kitchens of England were serving up.

Pottage and Ale; Food and Drink

A wide range of food was available in Tudor England, but few were able to afford it. Around sixty percent of the population was living at subsistence level and the difference in the diets between rich and poor was enormous.

The basic diet of the poor had barely changed since medieval times and would see little improvement for the next two hundred years or so. Most of what they ate consisted of bread and ale.

Water, especially in towns, was usually contaminated with human and animal waste and so weak ale was drunk instead, by all classes and even by children. This meant that huge quantities of ale had to be produced and most of it was brewed at home.

Bread was also eaten by all classes, but its quality varied considerably. The cheapest kind, maslin, was made with a mixture of rye and wheat flour, even pea flour or ground acorns when times were really hard. Manchett bread was of the best quality, made with sieved white wheat flour and fresh brewing yeast from the local alehouse. It was eaten only by the wealthier members of the community.

As with ale, there was a constant need to provide bread for the table. Until 1500 flour was usually milled at home, but this practice was eventually stopped by the mill owners who wanted to keep the business for themselves. It then became the custom for households to buy grain and take it to the local mill to be ground, rather than buying ready-made flour, which had a shorter shelf life. Many homes had no bread oven and so housewives had to take their prepared dough to the village baker to be baked for a fee. Finished loaves could also be bought from him.

Such heavy dependence on bread made the poor extremely vulnerable to shortages and crop failure. An especially dreadful situation developed during the 1550s when the wheat harvest failed for three years running. Famine spread throughout the country, killing hundreds of the poorest people. Scarcity led to a sharp increase in the price of grain, making things even worse.

Though bread was the basis of every meal, other food was available to folk on modest incomes. Cheese was eaten by all classes and country people drank the buttermilk and whey which were by-products of cheese and butter making. Nuts and herbs, depending on the season, could be found in hedgerows, and then there was pottage.

Pottage was a real staple of the ordinary person's diet. It was a kind of stew cooked in an earthenware pot over the fire ashes and was made with whatever was in season and available. A basic mixture of cereals, root vegetables and herbs could be improved with rabbit on a good day.

The Tudors before Henry VIII's Reformation were all Catholics. As such, they ate no meat on Fridays and Holy days and so large quantities of fish were required for the table. Ponds on monastery land produced fish for the local community who baked, fried or boiled it. It could also be preserved in salt for the winter, when no fresh fish was available. A variety of sauces flavoured with herbs and spices was often served with salt fish to make it more palatable.

Livestock rearing methods had been somewhat improved by the Tudor period. With the availability of winter fodder, animals could now be kept alive all year, rather than having to be slaughtered in autumn, as before. This led to a supply of fresh meat all year round and wealthier citizens were quick to take advantage of it.

Meat made up three quarters of the upper class menu. Oxen, deer, calves, pigs and wild boar were heartily consumed, as were chickens, pigeons and sparrows. For the aristocratic palette, there was also roasted peacock, presented in flamboyant style and decorated with its feathers. At court, swan or heron might also be served.

Meat was cooked in a variety of ways. In large households it could be roasted on spits before kitchen fires and served with rich, spicy sauces. Lesser cuts might be used in pies or stewed in iron cooking pots that were either hung from chains over the fire or placed over hot ashes.

The rich enjoyed sweet dishes prepared with expensive luxuries like dried fruit, almonds, spices and sugar. Sugar syrup was imported from Persia via Antwerp, where it was refined and made into sugar loaves. Cooks had to break pieces off the loaf and grind it using a pestle and mortar.

Being able to afford sugar was such a status symbol that a smile blackened by rotting teeth was proudly displayed by the wealthy. The upper classes were also developing a taste for expensive sweet imported wine, which was drunk between food courses. The most popular sweet reds were Malmsey and Romeyn, while Muscadel and Campole were favourite whites. Hippocras, a beverage made by straining wine several times through layers of spices, was also popular.

The lower classes did without sugar as few could afford it. Though they needed to preserve food over winter, modern preservation methods which rely on sugar, such as jam making or fruit bottling, were unavailable. Fruit and vegetables therefore had to keep by themselves. Bullace, quince and root vegetables were stored in cold attics or outhouses, while meat was preserved in tubs of salt water or smoked in chimneys.

However reliable this preservation was, winter fare for ordinary people was dull and unvaried, consisting mainly of pottage, bread, cheese and smoked bacon. If food was plentiful enough, though, this plain diet was considerably healthier than the meat and sugar rich choices of the upper classes.

Perhaps the most beneficial diet, however, was enjoyed by people half way down the social scale. Yeoman farmers raised their own animals for meat and milk and picked apples, pears, plums, strawberries and cherries from their own orchards. In summer they grew peas, beans, carrots and onions in their kitchen gardens and kept turnips for winter. Even their bread was made from home grown wheat. Because of their self-sufficiency, they probably purchased and ate less sugar than their wealthier neighbours.

Like her father Henry VIII, Queen Elizabeth enjoyed her food. Feasts held at court or in upper class homes were usually lavish affairs with a multitude of fine dishes. A typical first course might include brawn, tongue, leg of pork, pheasant, roast beef, venison, meat pies and bread. A second course would follow, perhaps of roast mutton, rabbit, tarts, jelly, custard and more bread.

Jelly was extremely popular, though laborious to make. Calves' feet had to be boiled for hours to produce the gelatine which was then clarified and flavoured with sugar, spices or wine. It was coloured using plants such as turnsole which, depending on its preparation, could produce shades of violet or red.

The way in which food was served had changed very little from medieval times. The different kinds of food were presented to the table on large platters called messes, each to be shared between four or six diners. Each diner had a napkin and a trencher. This was a large slice of bread used like a plate, but most food was simply taken from the mess using fingers and put straight into the mouth.

Each person brought their own knife and spoon to the table and shared a cup with the others in their group. Etiquette demanded, therefore, that they wiped their mouths on their napkin before drinking from the communal cup, to remove any grease and bits of food!

By the late Elizabethan period, a few changes had been introduced. Bread trenchers had mostly been replaced by wooden ones and the wealthy had begun to use small personal plates of silver or pewter. Pottery was sometimes used, but only for the large mess platters. Drinking vessels, which for the wealthy and fashionable had previously been of pewter, were gradually being replaced by glass. Fine Venetian vessels were by far the most expensive, costing five times as much as glasses produced elsewhere.

A third course called a banquet was also introduced to fashionable dining at this time. A banquet was a selection of sweets, nuts and cheese eaten at the end of a meal, away from the table. A new item of cutlery called a sweetmeat fork had been created for this culinary experience. It was used by diners to pick up delicate pieces of candied fruit to nibble on as they wandered around and enjoyed the house or grounds.

None of these changes affected the poor. They continued to drink from wooden beakers and to use their fingers to eat from wooden trenchers, though most folk had a knife for cutting and a spoon for pottage.

Queen Elizabeth was famous for her sweet tooth and had a fine set of blackened ones as a result. She added sugar to almost every dish and loved snacks of fruit, seeds and spices covered in sugar. Even her salads were laden with it.

There were healthier options, of course. Many seasonal fruits were available, strawberries being among the favourites. They were usually sweetened, though, with wine and sugar.

Ale continued to be drunk with every meal and could be flavoured with anything from garden herbs to the more exotic mace and nutmeg. During the late 1500s, however, a new flavouring arrived from Germany. The hops used to produce this flavour began to be grown in England and their popularity steadily grew. Called beer, this new hop enhanced drink would eventually become the standard form of ale.

Until the time of Elizabeth's reign, breakfast was eaten only by the labouring classes. For them it was a very early meal, eaten on waking at around 5am. The upper classes, meanwhile, generally rose much later in the day so had no need of breakfast. They didn't have long to wait until dinner, the main meal of the day, which was served at about 11am. Supper, a much simpler meal, followed at 5pm. Merchants and other prosperous, busy members of the middle classes tended to eat their meals a little later, to fit around their working day. They usually put back dinner to midday and supper to 6pm.

Now, however, breakfast was gaining popularity at court. It was a simple affair, consisting of little more than manchett bread, fish and meat. Although it must have been tricky at first to fit in an extra meal between rising and dinner, breakfast would gradually become part of the daily routine for all classes.

One of the later staples of the British diet first came to England during Elizabeth's reign. No one is quite sure who first brought the potato home from the Americas, but Francis Drake or one of his fellow privateers and adventurers are likely candidates. A herbal book published in 1597 by John Gerard devoted an entire chapter to the potato, newly arrived, as he understood it, from Virginia. Herbals such as Gerard's provided a lot of useful information for the many gardeners of the day who produced fruit and vegetables for their households in the newly fashionable kitchen gardens.

Tomatoes were introduced from Spain and Italy at around this time too. At first, they were believed to be poisonous, so their use in cookery didn't really start until the mid eighteenth century.

The warfare that blighted much of the seventeenth century led to few changes in eating habits. It wasn't until the monarchy was restored under Charles II in 1660 that new ideas once again flourished.

His reign was one of innovation and fresh thinking which affected all aspects of daily life. Coffee houses had begun to appear in London in around 1650 and they soon became enormously popular throughout the whole country.

Coffee houses served not only coffee, but drinking chocolate and even tea. They were strictly for men only, though women were allowed to work in them. The cost for entry, including one cup of coffee or chocolate, was one old penny and gentlemen met there to discuss anything from politics and business to the latest gossip.

Tea, however, was the most fashionable beverage of the time. Imported from China by the East India Company, it was so expensive that it was enjoyed only by the very rich.

Serving tea in the great houses of England became something of a ceremony, the hostess herself brewing it and serving it to her guests after dinner. She poured hot water from a small silver kettle on to tea leaves in a fashionable porcelain tea pot. Tea was served black with sugar and could be drunk either from a porcelain tea bowl or its saucer. These delicately designed tea pots, handleless tea bowls and matching saucers were imported from China and were extremely popular.

English ceramic factories would take many years to perfect a method for creating porcelain. In the meantime, they produced heavy earthenware tankards and platters for the home. Large tin-glazed delftware plates, colourfully decorated with images of the king, were cheerful additions to home decor, but were vastly inferior to Chinese porcelain.

Samuel Pepys' first experience of tea drinking was faithfully recorded in his diary in September 1660, when he described the beverage as 'a China drink.'

Amongst Pepys' detailed narrative concerning his business and home life, are descriptions of social occasions. In January 1663 he wrote about a dinner he and his wife gave for seven guests. His wife went out early to the market to shop for food and his guests arrived later that morning.

After a first course of oysters, the party enjoyed a hash of rabbits and lamb and a rare chine of beef.

'Next,' he wrote, 'a great dish of roasted fowl, cost me about thirty shillings, and a tart, and then fruit and cheese.... I had my house mighty clean and neat; my room below with a good fire in it; my dining-room above, and my chamber made a with-drawing-chamber....I find my new table very proper, and will hold nine or ten people well...'

Later, they had supper with 'a good sack posset and cold meat' and his guests left at ten o'clock. He declared the event a success.

He seems temporarily to have turned his chamber into a fashionable drawing room for his guests' use after dinner. The sack he refers to was white fortified Spanish wine and a sack posset was hot milk with something similar to sherry added.

The later Stuarts saw the arrival of some interesting inventions. In 1682, for instance, a French doctor called Denys Papin invented the pressure cooker. To demonstrate the efficiency of his invention, he prepared a meal of fish, beef, mutton and pigeons for several guests. Using low heat, he steamed the food in its own juices and explained that his pressure cooker was also excellent for preserving fruit. It seems the demonstration was a success, but it would be quite some time before it gained popularity.

Adequate nutrition was, of course, essential for the nation's health, but medicine and hygiene were equally important. Which is a subject in itself.

Rosemary; you have been warned!

Abracadabra; Health and Hygiene

Medical knowledge in early Tudor England was rather thin on the ground. A general lack of understanding about the causes of disease was made worse by poor sanitation and low standards of hygiene. It is hardly surprising that the average life expectancy was so low; age thirty-two for men and thirty-five for women. It was quite usual for the poor to die in their twenties.

Within the monasteries, monks had kept themselves clean as part of their religious discipline, but not everyone at that time had paid so much attention to bodily hygiene. The age-old fear that immersing the body in water would open pores in the skin and let in infection, did not help.

Rather than wash their bodies, therefore, anyone with more than one set of underclothes laundered and changed them regularly. Underwear was made of linen which was good for absorbing sweat, grease and dirt from the body, so regular washing of linen shirts, smocks, hose, ruffs, cuffs and caps did a lot to prevent body odour.

Wash day for most households, though, came round just once a month. Even by the 1660s, the diarist Samuel Pepys wrote about his wife and their maid doing the 'monthly wash'. When it occurred, however, it was labour intensive. Lye, made from wood ash, was used to soak the linen before it was washed, wrung out and spread on the grass to dry.

Fine and expensive clothing of wool and silk was rarely, if ever, washed. This applied also to naturally dyed fabrics and any garment decorated with beadwork or embroidery. These clothes were kept fragrant when not being worn by inserting bags of herbs between their folds.

Stains were removed in a variety of ways. Depending on the type of stain, alkaline lye, acidic lemon juice, absorbent fuller's earth or dispersants like alcohol and egg white were used. When the linings of gowns and doublets became too marked with sweat, they were taken out and replaced. Velvets and certain other types of fabric were brushed to keep them looking good.

In total contrast, the very poor, who owned but one set of clothes, had practically no chance of keeping themselves clean.

Despite a general reluctance to wash the body, there was plenty of common sense applied to cleaning the home. The rushes covering the floor were changed at least twice a year, as after a while the old ones became dirty and infested with vermin. Sweet smelling herbs were strewn on the floors beneath the fresh rushes, to combat unpleasant odours. It was generally believed that disease was spread by bad smells, so herbs were considered a good deterrent.

It was especially important for the dairy to be kept clean. Salt was used on a damp cloth to scour work surfaces and milk pans. Boiling water was then used to rinse every surface, bowl and pan before leaving the items outside to dry, weather permitting. Although no one at the time knew about bacteria, these methods were efficient means of killing it. Instinct and the knowledge of what had worked in the past kept dairies clean for producing the milk, cream, butter and cheese which were essential to the working man and woman's diet.

No matter what a person's attitude to hygiene was, everyone was vulnerable to disease. One of the most feared illnesses was the Sweating Sickness. It is believed now to have been a very severe form of influenza which caused profuse sweating, high fever, dizziness and severe pain in the head and abdomen. The Sweating Sickness could strike anywhere and is thought to have caused the death of Prince Arthur, the son of Henry VII, in 1502. There were many other outbreaks of this sickness during the 1400s and 1500s which killed thousands of people.

Dysentery and Typhus were also rife, but affected mostly the lower classes. Dysentery, also known as the Flux, could be picked up by drinking dirty water. Typhus was spread by the lice, fleas and ticks which abounded on the unwashed bodies of the poorest people. Then of course there were the bubonic and pneumonic plagues which cast their deadly shadows over Britain and Europe for centuries.

Childbirth carried a huge risk. The death rate for both the mother and child was high, yet healthy women still managed to give birth to many children. Despite this, few families were large. Only about half the number of babies made it to the age of five.

Trying to combat all of this sickness and disease were the physicians, surgeons and apothecaries. However well educated, the medical knowledge of physicians was still very limited and based on beliefs that seem peculiar today. They thought that the health of the human body relied on the balance of four humours; sanguine, choleric, phlegmatic and melancholic. Their attempts to balance the humours all too often relied on blood-letting and purging, frequently making a sick patient even weaker.

Surgeons could be called upon to amputate limbs, though this was always as a last resort, since the work was carried out without anaesthetic. Apothecaries sold herbal cures, but these too were based on the theory of the four humours.

The fees charged by physicians and the high cost of orthodox medicine, however, made them unavailable to the poor. Once the monasteries and religious guilds had gone, together with their infirmaries and almshouses, the penniless were left largely to fend for themselves. Their only resort was to the local wise women who for centuries had been offering their own brand of cures and herbal concoctions. Their skills were needed especially during childbirth, where their experience and inherited wisdom made them far more useful than male physicians.

Some of their cures were a little strange, though. Latin incantations formed part of their rituals, to add an air of mystery to their work. They also produced charms to ward off evil.

One charm involved the writing of the Hebrew word for 'Abracadabra' in full on a scrap of paper. The word was written again underneath, but with one letter missing. Beneath that, it was repeated again with a further letter missed out. Continuing down and gradually forming an inverted pyramid shape, the word was repeated with another letter dropped each time until a single Hebrew letter remained at the bottom. The paper bearing this magical word, thought now to be a misinterpretation of 'Father, Son and Holy Spirit', was carried around to ward off ill luck.

Other remedies were truly bizarre. Spiders were believed to be effective in the treatment of ague (malaria), so living spiders were held in little pouches and worn around the neck. Even less fortunately for the spiders, some were swallowed alive. There were many people in the Fens who believed they had been cured of the ague using such methods and it wasn't just the poor and uneducated who had faith in them. The antiquarian and founding Fellow of the Royal Academy, Elias Ashmole, recorded in his diary of 1681 that he'd hung three spiders around his neck and that they had driven away his ague.

Back in 1518, years before the Reformation and destruction of monastic hospitals, Henry VIII had established the Royal College of Physicians. He had been attempting to rid the country of its many quacks and charlatans who passed themselves off as experts and did more harm than good. The college president, Thomas Linacre, was empowered to fine or imprison anyone found practising without proper qualifications.

This is thought to have been the first formal control of medicine in England. The college continued to develop and in 1586 a physic garden was planted there, so that the use of plants in medicine could be further researched.

These measures did not affect anyone practising as a surgeon. Unlike physicians, surgeons were not required to have any formal education and the amputations and bloodletting they carried out won them little respect. In 1540, however, a move was made to raise their status. Two guilds, that of the Barbers' Company established in 1461 and the Guild of Surgeons, joined forces to create the new College of Barbers and Surgeons. This enabled students to be better trained and the king granted them his approval in the form of a charter.

The wealthiest Tudors, though protected from many of the health risks threatening the poor, invited problems of their own. During Elizabeth's reign, ladies followed their queen's example in using make-up containing poisonous mercury and lead on their skin. In an equally ill advised way, the upper classes ate so much sugar that it rotted their teeth. Queen Elizabeth, with her painted white face and mouthful of blackened teeth, was unconsciously poisoning herself.

Tooth decay led to bad breath among other problems, so the queen stepped up her daily dental regime to combat the problem. Each morning she is said to have rinsed out her mouth with fresh water fragranced with cinnamon or myrrh before her ladies in waiting cleaned her teeth. To remove stains they used soot, sometimes combined with salt as an abrasive. A mixture of white wine and vinegar, boiled with honey, was also rubbed on the teeth using a fine cloth. Rather than helping, this treatment must have damaged the queen's dental health even further. During the day, she is said to have chewed herbs to keep her breath fresh and to have used disposable toothpicks to remove stray pieces of food.

Elizabeth's reign saw a number of valiant efforts to improve sanitation. In 1582 a Dutchman by the name of Pieter Morice invented a system for pumping water from the River Thames into London. His pumps were powered by a large water wheel housed under an arch of London Bridge. His invention was a success and was used for many years, pleasing everyone but the water carriers, who had until then been the principal means of bringing water into London.

In 1596, a courtier and poet and one of Queen Elizabeth's many god sons, Sir John Harington, invented the first flushable toilet. His diagrams showing how a water closet was constructed were published in his book, 'The Metamorphosis of Ajax'. This new facility, known as an Ajax (from 'jakes', old slang for a loo), had a flush valve to release water from a tank into the toilet bowl and a clever system for emptying the bowl. He had a water closet installed in his own home and it is said that the queen herself had one, but it would be a long time before such things became the norm.

Care and nursing in the community was still seriously lacking and the fate of aged and injured ex-soldiers was particularly worrying to the queen. Robert Dudley, the Earl of Leicester and the queen's favourite, rose to the challenge and founded what would become known as the Lord Leycester Hospital in Warwick. It was not a hospital in the modern sense, more a home for retired soldiers and their wives, but still a very useful facility. The foundation was run by twelve resident brethren under the supervision of a master and was funded by income from some of the earl's estates. It is still there today.

In later years Oliver Cromwell founded institutions for the care of wounded and sick soldiers on active service. Before then, the injured had been billeted at inns, a situation which was far from satisfactory. After the restoration of the monarchy, Charles II built on this idea with the founding of the Chelsea Hospital in 1682. The hospital for seamen at Greenwich followed in 1696.

The seventeenth century was a time of new thinking and research into health and medicine. In 1604, King James I made remarks about smoking which would hardly be out of place in modern newspapers. Tobacco had arrived in England from the Americas during the Elizabethan era and the smoking of clay pipes had become enormously popular among the upper classes. The habit had quickly spread to the ale houses and both men and women smoked pipes, believing that tobacco was good for them. It was said to relieve toothache, worms, bad breath and many other complaints.

The new king, however, found smoking repugnant and publicised his opinions in a pamphlet called 'A Counterblaste to Tobacco'. He believed smoking to be harmful to the lungs, unpleasant to the eye and to the nose. No one seems to have taken much notice, though. Tobacco grew even more popular and by the late 1600s was also taken by gentlemen in the powdered form of snuff.

Also doing his best to promote good health was the physician, astrologer and herbalist Nicholas Culpepper. In 1640 he established his premises in Red Lion Street, Spitalfields.

Although he relied heavily on astrology in his work, his extensive cataloguing of plants and their properties earned him great respect. The books he published, including 'The Complete Herbal' became pharmaceutical text books. He made many interesting observations. Duck weed, for example, was good for gout, while rosemary was helpful for 'windiness in the stomach, bowels and spleen, and expels it powerfully'. You have been warned!

The death rate during the Stuart period, despite all the available remedies, remained high. The deaths that occurred in each parish were carefully recorded, even though sometimes very little was known about the deceased. The lack of identity of some, and the brief notes about others which appear in the Wisbech Registers of the early 1700s, make rather sad reading. The following are just a few examples:

1713, 24th January: Elizabeth, a stranger.
1714, 21st August: A stranger unknown.
1719, 21st October: Faith, Hope and Charity, daughters of Richard Watson.
1720, 1st October: Robert Pevison, a comedian.
1741, 20th August: An Irishman.
1741, 10th December: Child left at Captain Norris' door.

On that sobering note, perhaps it is time to lighten things up a bit and look at how people dressed themselves.

Red Heels and Farthingales; What They Wore

Fashion changed enormously during the two hundred years or so of the Tudors and Stuarts. Describing every trend would take way too long, so the following is just a quick look at the main shapes and developments for each era.

Men

Early Tudor clothing was still basically medieval. The main components of a gentleman's attire, the doublet, jerkin, hose and gown, would remain as staples for years to come, with only minor variations in length, shape and detail.

It was Henry VIII and his boisterous, larger-than-life personality who influenced the first significant development in Tudor male costume. The whole shape became wider, emphasised by broad shouldered, short gowns. Beneath the gown was worn the jerkin, which, a little like a modern jacket, was long enough to cover the upper legs. The doublet was worn under the jerkin and, next to the skin, the linen shirt.

The hose, which were attached with ties to the doublet, were full and pouched at the top, narrowing to a close fit on the lower legs. Very exaggerated codpieces completed this macho and swaggering look.

Shoes were wide and square toed; boots were used only for riding. Hats called bonnets were shaped like soft caps with turned-down brims, sometimes trimmed with a brooch or feather.

Always keen to keep people in their place, Henry introduced a Sumptuary Law in 1532. Among its dictates was a ruling on which furs could be worn by the different classes. Sable, for example, could only be worn by the royal family, leaving the nobility to make do with ermine, rabbit, squirrel and wolf skin. Even colours were restricted. Only royalty and the nobility were entitled to wear deep crimson and anything with gold embroidery.

As the king aged, fashion altered to suit him. The neckline of the linen shirt became higher and the doublet lengthened to show off less leg.

But such high fashion was worn only by the moneyed upper classes. The professional middle classes kept to more practical styles. Merchants, priests, lawyers and older men in general wore long, loose, black robes over their jerkin, doublet and hose.

Fashion had very little effect on the clothing of the poor. Their tunics and breeches were of hard wearing woollen cloth in shades of blue or brown from vegetable based dyes. A baggy linen shirt was worn next to the skin and woollen stockings covered the lower legs. Shoes usually consisted of wooden clogs or were made of coarse leather. The very poor went barefoot.

Most of the clothing worn by the poor was homemade, though second hand garments could be bought cheaply from dealers called fripperers.

Development of a gentleman's costume from (left) c.1530 to (right) c.1630

The later 1500s were dominated by glamorous new fashion influenced by Queen Elizabeth I.

The basic components of a gentleman's wardrobe acquired a new shape. The doublet became much longer and was padded at the front to form a 'peasecod belly', finishing in a V-shape which fitted neatly over the trunk hose. The hose were padded with horsehair at the top to cover the hips and upper leg, narrowing as before to fit the leg tightly from the thigh to the foot.

Hose and stockings, which had until then been made of woven cloth, could now also be knitted. By 1560, knitting had become an important craft for both men and women who produced a multitude of stockings, caps and gloves.

The jerkin, worn as before over the doublet, was sometimes fashioned from leather. Gowns were generally long and lined with velvet or fox fur, but a more dashing appearance could be achieved with a short, full cloak, worn in the way of characters like Sir Walter Raleigh.

The taffeta, satin, brocade or velvet used to create these fine garments was dyed black or an array of bright yellows, reds and blues. Fabric was heavily embroidered. Steel sewing needles had been developed, replacing old ones of drawn wire. The new needles were stronger and led to a huge increase in embroidery, cut-work and lace.

Shoes were of fine Spanish leather, silk or velvet and were flat until about 1600. Higher heels then came into fashion, a wedge of cork or leather inserted under the heel to achieve the effect.

Topping all this magnificence and giving it a truly Elizabethan look, was the ruff. Fairly modest to begin with, ruffs were attached to the neck of the linen shirt and made of lace- trimmed cambric or lawn. Initially they were held in shape with strips of bone, but after 1564, when starch was introduced into England, ruffs really came into their own. They could then be stiffened into complex, huge, and probably uncomfortable, grandeur.

Hats changed too, higher crowned beaver headwear taking over from flat bonnets. Hair was cut short and worn with a neatly pointed beard.

Little boys wore petticoats like their sisters until the age of six, when they were 'breeched'. They were then dressed in mini versions of adult clothing with knee length, loose fitting breeches.

With the early Stuarts came a new look. Gone was the exaggerated padding of Elizabethan times, replaced by a longer shape and breeches that reached the knees. The doublet was finished in a V-shape at the front which fitted over the breeches and the two garments were often made as a suit in matching fabrics.

From around 1615 a new 'falling ruff' gradually replaced Elizabethan versions. The new ruff consisted of two or three layers of lace-edged linen or lawn that formed a deep collar-like band around the high-necked doublet.

Round toed shoes were decorated with bows or rosettes and high heels of cork or wood continued in popularity. Wooden heels were dyed red for full court dress, a tradition which would continue until the late 1700s.

Wide brimmed, high crowned beaver or felt hats were often swept up on one side and trimmed with a feather. Hats were still worn indoors, even at meals and in church, but were removed in the presence of the king.

During the reign of Charles I, as trouble brewed between parliament and the crown, supporters of each side began to favour their own distinct style of clothing.

Men loyal to the king, especially the nobility and upper classes, opted for colourful, extravagant styles. Parliamentary supporters, meanwhile, who were typically middle class and many of them Puritans, favoured more modest clothing in subdued shades.

For well dressed royalists, a new wide, lace-trimmed collar dominated a much more loosely tailored doublet than before. Usually worn open, the doublet displayed the shirt beneath and was attached to the breeches. These were fairly tight fitting, reaching to below the knee where they were gartered and decorated with huge bows. White silk stockings covered the lower leg.

Shoes for formal dress, which still favoured red heels, were square toed and decorated with large bows, while hats were more extravagant than ever. Their wide brims, still swept up on one side, were trimmed with large ostrich plumes.

Parliamentary supporters tended to wear toned down versions of this costume. Wealthier Puritans favoured plain black garments, but black dye was expensive and folk on smaller incomes settled for shades of brown. Their hair was cut short, in distinct contrast to the bearded, long haired looks of the royalists. In some cases it was so closely cropped that it earned them the name of Roundheads. Their hats were high crowned and untrimmed, their doublets and hose simply cut and finished with plain white linen collars.

During the time of the Protectorate, the sober dress of the Puritans was gradually adopted by all. After eleven years, the restoration of the monarchy must have come as a great relief, if only to the fashion conscious.

Charles II led a national rejection of restraint. A completely new style of clothing was introduced which reflected this new mood.

The doublet, that mainstay of male costume for centuries, was no more. Instead, the shirt was covered by a long waistcoat which reached to just above the knees. A loose fitting coat of the same length covered the waistcoat, almost hiding the very full breeches beneath. Gathered into a band at the knee, they were decorated with loops of ribbon called 'fancies'. Collars were gradually replaced by cravats, finished with a bow at the front.

Wigs became very fashionable. Men cut their own hair short and covered their heads with long periwigs of curly hair. These were topped by low crowned, wide brimmed hats.

The later Stuarts introduced small changes in fashion, but nothing as significant as that of Charles II. Shorter versions of the periwig, tied in a ponytail, were adopted by the military, though long wigs continued to be worn by everyone else. When they were removed indoors, small linen caps were used to cover short hair or shaved heads. Although hats altered very little, it became unacceptable for them to be worn indoors.

King Charles had, in reclaiming the crown, reintroduced flair in design to all walks of life. With it had come a completely new look which replaced the doublet and hose that had dominated male costume for over two hundred years.

It was a look which would be developed and built on throughout the Georgian period.

Women

A Tudor lady's costume, in a way similar to a gentleman's, consisted of a few basic items which changed only in a minor way for years. These were the linen shift, the kirtle and the gown.

The linen shift, together with woollen stockings gartered above the knee, were all a lady wore as underwear. Over the shift went the kirtle, a full length under-dress with long sleeves, usually laced up at the back. The gown, the most important item of all, and the one which altered most with every fashion change, was the top layer, worn over the kirtle.

Development of a lady's costume from (left) c.1530 to (right) c.1630

At the court of Henry VIII tightly fitted bodices with low, square necklines dictated the fashionable shape of gown. Skirts of taffeta, velvet, silk, satin or damask were long and trailing and held their full shape with the aid of a layered petticoat beneath the kirtle. The sleeves, bodice and skirt of the gown were not sewn together, but held in place with steel pins.

Headdresses were called hoods. The gable hood, which was popular during the early years of Henry's reign, framed the face and a veil at the back covered the hair. During the 1530s, fashionable ladies abandoned the gable in favour of a rounded shape of hood. The French hood, newly arrived from the continent, was set further back on the head and showed some of the hair at the front.

Lower down the social scale, the clothing of middle class women was far more practical. Even for fairly well placed women, it was unusual to own more than a couple of gowns and these were highly prized items. Worn over the kirtle, they were generally finished with a long hanging belt called a girdle. Hoods tended to be of the gabled variety, even after the fashion at court had moved on.

The value placed on these garments is indicated by the Will of Elizabeth Fisher of Tydd St Giles, mentioned in Chapter Two. On her death in 1524 she left, among her most valued possessions, her best gown, kirtle, belt and linen cap to a servant.

But the vast majority of the female population, the ordinary working women of Tudor England, dressed far more simply. Their long kirtles of coarse wool covered shifts of homespun linen and knee length woollen stockings. They were very unlikely to own a gown. Their hair, rarely washed, was covered with a linen cap or a veil. Shoes, if they could afford them, were not dissimilar to men's; usually clogs or coarse leather items. For warmth in winter they added long woollen cloaks.

Queen Elizabeth, in her own feminine way, was as ostentatious as her father, Henry VIII, had been. Whereas his huge personality had influenced male fashion to outshine female, under Elizabeth it was the opposite; female costume now blossomed.

Large neck ruffs, wide-hipped skirts and richly embroidered garments made ladies' fashion some of the most extravagant of all time.

The shape of Elizabethan costume was achieved by the long bodice and wide A-line of the skirt. Buttons now replaced ties for fastening the bodice at the back and stays of wood or whalebone were used to keep its rigid form. The farthingale, a structural petticoat with hoops sewn into it, held the skirt in shape.

Sleeves were tight at the wrist, but swelled out towards the shoulder and were so heavily padded that it was almost impossible for a lady to move her arms. This limitation on physical activity became a status symbol; anyone so incapable of movement needed plenty of servants and so had to be rich!

A new shape of farthingale introduced between 1580 and 1620 supported a completely new shape of gown. The French farthingale was a padded roll worn around the hips and tied at the front. There were several variations, but one of the most distinctive made the skirt stand out around the hips and back, but kept it flat at the front.

Just about everything was embroidered; velvet, silk, taffeta and satin gowns and petticoats, even shoes. Ribbons were used to tie shoes at the front and cork wedges were inserted to heighten the heel.

The heavy fabrics fashionable at that time must have been very welcome in winter. With temperatures dropping regularly to around two degrees lower than today, ladies added extra woollen layers beneath the finer outer fabric of the gown.

Queen Elizabeth could be said to have begun the custom of hat wearing for women. Before her time, married women had invariably covered their hair with veils or hoods, but now they wore the kind of hats favoured by men. At first, these were modest affairs with small brims and low crowns, but it was a start. Things would never go back.

The queen encouraged women to display their hair more than before. Girls and unmarried young women began to wear their hair long and uncovered, even out of doors.

As the queen aged, fashion was adapted to flatter her. Elizabeth needed dye, false hair and finally full wigs to maintain an illusion of youth, and the fashion of the 1590s followed suit. Hair was dressed high on the head using hidden pads and false hair, and toxic white lead make-up was used on the face.

In an attempt to prevent the beauty of her female courtiers surpassing her fading looks, Elizabeth's government passed the Nine Acts of Apparel in 1574. Similar sumptuary laws had been imposed by monarchs in the past to dictate the kind of clothing that could be worn by the different ranks. This was the first time, however, that ladies, as well as gentlemen, had been told how to dress.

The reign of James I, the first of the Stuarts, saw the introduction of a completely new style of gown, one which would dominate fashion for the next fifty years, or so. Old, cumbersome farthingales were discarded in favour of a much simpler look. The waist was set higher and the skirts, now sewn to the bodice rather than being pinned, hung unencumbered from the waist to the hem. Sleeves were shorter and fuller and finished with deep linen cuffs.

Largely replacing the ruff, a wide lace-trimmed 'falling collar' accompanied the new gowns. Unbroken at the front, the collar formed a lacy, fan-like semi-circle which partly filled the very low, U-shaped neckline.

Hair was far more simply styled, brushed back from the forehead and coiled into a bun at the back. The hair at the sides was loosely curled. For formal occasions, it was decorated with ribbons, feathers, even jewels, and the folding fan first seen at Elizabeth's court often accompanied the look. The most fashionable ladies stuck little black velvet patches on their faces with mastic, believing them to be alluring.

Under James' son, Charles I, who came to the throne in 1625, fashion began to be influenced by politics. As with men, supporters of parliament and the king adopted very different styles.

Even if wealthy, female supporters of parliament gravitated towards plain gowns in dark colours, trimmed with white linen cuffs. The middle classes continued to wear small ruffs at first, but these were gradually replaced by plain white linen collars. A cap of the same plain material covered the hair and a new, high crowned 'Puritan hat' was worn by many.

For royalists, life was a lot more stylish. Members of the nobility and upper classes continued to dress in brightly coloured satin, silk and taffeta. Necklines were low and square, both at the front and back, to display the neck. Waistlines were even higher than before and the puffed sleeves were shorter and trimmed with ribbons. Elbow length, tightly fitting gloves were worn with them.

Large brimmed 'Cavalier hats' of velvet, trimmed with a large feather, became very popular for riding.

During the Protectorate, when Puritan tastes influenced the way everyone dressed, even ladies with secretly royalist leanings moderated their costume. Fabrics were dyed in subdued shades of grey, blue, violet and black and low necklines were disguised by large scarves draped across the shoulders. Ladies even adopted the 'Puritan hat', though many trimmed it with feathers to make it more interesting.

The restoration of the monarchy meant that beautiful clothes could be worn again. Puritan hats and linen collars were hastily discarded, replaced by glamorous, colourful new gowns. Necklines widened once more, becoming low and rounded, while bodices were stiffened with bone stays to emphasise tiny waists. Skirts were full and sometimes swept back to display the petticoat beneath.

Hair, worn in ringlets and coiled into a bun at the back, was mostly uncovered. Only when riding were wide brimmed hats worn.

High heeled shoes of brocade or embroidered satin became more feminine and slender in shape. Black velvet beauty spots came back into fashion and would remain there for decades.

Not everyone, of course, followed the new fashion. The elderly, the poor and women whose religious views found more comfort in simplicity, continued with their tall hats, linen collars and plain clothes.

The reign of William and Mary saw the introduction of the bustle and a new, high headdress, which gave the figure a completely different and distinctive shape.

The skirt became much narrower at the front, its sides fastened back to reveal the decorative petticoat beneath and forming a small bustle at the back. This slimmer shape was emphasised by the height of the headdress. Folds of linen and lace were arranged on a tall frame which sat forward on the head, a small cap covering the hair at the back. In winter a hood was worn over the cap, behind the towering headdress. By 1700, any hair managing to peep out at the front was powdered.

The tall headdress would fall out of fashion after a mere fifteen years, but powdered hair would be seen more and more in the Georgian period to come. Once more, fashion was on the brink of change.

For the vast majority of English people, though, clothing was simply a necessity and style had nothing to do with it. What really mattered to them was putting food on the table and the work they did to put it there.

The Taylor memorial in St Peter's Church showing 16th century Puritan clothing (with permission of the parish church)

Dawn to Sunset; Work

The Church provided a huge amount of employment for the early Tudors. Henry VIII's dissolution of the monasteries ended all of that, leaving thousands of monastic servants without work and shelter and with nowhere to go.

Some of the more able bodied were offered work by yeoman farmers, but as monastery after monastery closed down, poverty and homelessness reached crisis point.

Other problems contributed to this national crisis. Sheep farming and the wool trade had become the greatest source of employment in many rural areas, including East Anglia. The trouble with this was that fewer workers were needed for sheep rearing than for agriculture, and more and more land once used for crops was being turned into pasture. This was a logical move for land owners because sheep farming was enormously profitable and they needed to pay fewer workers. It was, however, steadily increasing the number of unemployed.

The problems did not end there. During the early 1500s an increasing acreage of woodland and meadow land was fenced off to keep sheep in. This enclosed land then became out of bounds for local people.

For centuries, villagers had relied on the right to graze their animals on common land. Their pigs had been allowed to forage in woodland for acorns and beech mast, and folk had been able to gather firewood and other materials from the common. This access to common land was essential to their livelihood and had been accepted for centuries as their right.

The land owners who enclosed this land cared nothing for traditional rights and usually the authorities did nothing to stop them. In most cases this left nowhere for the villagers' animals to graze and hunger soon followed. Desperate to earn a living, many people left the countryside for the towns and some villages were abandoned altogether.

There were landowners who went still further in the ill treatment of their poorer neighbours. As the conversion of agricultural land into pasture grew more profitable, some smallholdings and cottages on large estates, many of which had been rented by the same family for generations, were suddenly seen as in the way. Rather than renewing tenancy agreements when they became due, eviction notices were issued. Cottages were demolished to clear space for more pasture, leaving the smallholders homeless and without alternative means to support themselves.

It wasn't long before the reduction in agricultural land led to food shortages and inflation. This finally prompted Henry VIII to act and in 1534 a new law banned any one farmer from owning more than two thousand sheep. This, it was hoped, would limit the growth of the huge estates dedicated to sheep farming and reduce rural depopulation. It must have come as a shock to some East Anglian land owners who kept as many as twenty thousand animals at the time.

The new law went some way to alleviating the situation, but royal concerns about rural decay, inflation and poverty were not immediately assuaged. In 1548, the new king, Edward VI, ordered a commission to look into land enclosure and the problems it was creating.

On a more positive note, the highly profitable wool trade prompted many people to learn to spin and weave. These ancient crafts had changed very little since medieval times. Wool and flax were spun on large domestic spinning wheels, while weaving had been made a little easier by the introduction of large timber-built looms. Before the dissolution, these looms had been owned by the monasteries and used on a fee basis by local people. After the religious houses had been confined to history, new private landlords had taken over the ownership of the looms.

The loom held the warp threads lengthwise in tension, separating them to allow the shuttle, which held the weft thread, to be passed horizontally through them. The cloth this produced was quite flat in texture and had to be pounded using a fulling machine, another landowner-run facility, to make a thicker fabric.

Other essential crafts were carried out in village and town workshops. Potters produced earthenware platters and cooking pots, cobblers made leather shoes, and saddlers produced leather buckets and harnesses, as well as saddles. Carpenters crafted furniture, doors, windows, carts, wooden plates and cups. In their smithies, blacksmiths created knives, tools and weapons, as well as a huge number of horseshoes. Horses were central to Tudor and Stuart life and needed iron horseshoes to enable them to travel long distances and to pull carts, ploughs and harrows.

Tailors, who sewed garments for the middle and upper classes, were more likely to set up their workshops in town, where there was more business. Typically sitting cross-legged on the floor to sew, they used a variety of tools including shears, chalk, parchment, a yardstick, pins, needles, thread and a thimble.

Lesser skilled work for countrymen included ditch digging, ploughing, harvesting, hay cutting and the care of livestock. Peasants might also work as builders, labourers or thatchers.

An apprenticeship was the usual way in which a young man learned a trade. Depending on the trade he was learning, he might work on a farm, in a workshop or a private house, but invariably he lived with the master craftsman until fully trained.

Though the religious guilds had been dissolved by Edward VI, craft guilds continued as an important part of Tudor and Stuart life. Guilds protected the interests of their members, the master craftsmen. They provided financial help to sick brethren and to the widows and orphans of deceased members. They also carried out strict quality control on their members' work and could expel anyone for dishonesty or the production of overpriced or inferior goods. Once shamed in this way, a master craftsman would no longer be able to continue trading in that town.

Each guild had its own livery, proudly worn by its members. The bakers' guild, for example, had livery of green and maroon, the basket makers' white and blue.

A master craftsman was one who had reached the height of excellence in his own particular craft and had become a member of the guild. He could then take on apprentices. The apprentice's family paid for his training, which often went on for as long as seven years. The master was not permitted to train his own son, however, having to entrust his children to other craftsmen. When an apprentice was fully trained he became a journeyman. He could then enter employment, usually continuing with the master who had trained him. Through experience and hard work he could eventually join the guild as a master craftsman in his own right.

Boys who could read and write might aspire to becoming clerks, printers, book binders or book sellers. With a higher level of education, they could aim to be bankers, priests or teachers. Young men with a university education could train to become doctors or lawyers.

For girls, the choice was far more restricted. Daughters were generally taught to cook, clean, spin and weave by their mothers from an early age. Depending on the family's social standing and income, girls might also work on the land, in dairies, or become laundresses, children's nurses or ladies' maids.

It wasn't unusual for a widow to continue to run her late husband's business. Inn keepers, drapers and tradespeople of many other kinds were often women.

The poorest people, though, simply became servants. Girls and boys from about the age of fourteen, whose parents could not afford apprenticeships for them, went to work as household servants.

Their wages were small, as they were also provided with board and lodging. Often, there was no social distinction between them and the family they worked for. Everyone simply toiled together to manage the arduous everyday tasks of running a home or a smallholding. It was usual for servants to share beds with the family's children, who in later years were likely to become servants themselves, in other homes.

The greatest source of employment in Wisbech was the port, and its prosperity spread throughout the local economy. It wasn't just the boat crews and quayside workers who found work there. Sail makers, rope makers, carpenters, chandlers and blacksmiths also thrived and in turn they supported other town businesses, such as inns and suppliers of foodstuff, clothes and household goods.

The neighbouring port of King's Lynn, however, was enjoying an even greater level of prosperity. During the reign of Elizabeth I many of its wealthy merchants built large homes and warehouses on the quayside. One of these was Clifton House. Though parts of the house are medieval, its five storey tower is a reminder of its Elizabethan past. The structure's great height made it invaluable as a watch tower and its well furnished rooms were used for business. The tower remains an attractive land mark in King's Lynn today.

New regulations, meanwhile, were affecting working conditions all over the country. The Statute of Artificers of 1563 was not the first Act which had attempted to regulate earnings, but it *was* the first to regulate working hours and conditions too. Its aim was to banish idleness in young workers. Considering that some were as young as ten, these new rules seem harsh by modern standards.

The working day for boys and young men employed in agriculture now officially began at 5am and ended at 7pm in summer. In winter, they worked from dawn to sunset. The day was broken up by meal breaks totalling two and a half hours. A daily wage of sixpence was usual and any boy failing to turn up for work could be reported to the local Justice of the Peace, who had the right to fine him.

As another example of official influence affecting the workplace, the Stationers' Company was granted a royal charter in 1557 which gave it the monopoly for printing and publishing in England. Originally, stationers were also book sellers, printers and publishers. Their name came from the stations or stalls they set up in cathedral precincts, such as in St Paul's Churchyard in London.

Books were expensive luxuries, available only to the wealthy. Every aspect of their production was labour intensive. The paper was made from soaked linen rags, each sheet formed in a frame then left to dry. The printing process was very time consuming, each word constructed with metal 'sorts', or small letter blocks. The printed pages had then to be cut, sewn together and bound in a leather cover. The resulting high cost was kept even more exclusive by the ruling that only 1,250 copies could be printed of each edition. This was done to keep the stationers in employment.

Towards the end of Elizabeth's reign, London shopping was given almost a modern touch. The new shopping arcade called Gresham's Royal Exchange allowed people to wander from shop to shop, protected from the weather and the muddy streets outside. Gresham's had two floors of kiosks selling shoes, watches, silks, gloves and many other things. A few years later, the New Exchange was opened on the Strand, also with kiosks on two levels. This new shopping experience was good for both traders and the well-to-do who browsed and bought there.

Shortly afterwards, another service with a modern touch was introduced. Introduced by King Charles I in the 1630s, the postal service was very basic to start with. Letters were taken by mounted couriers along designated routes marked by posts, or delivery points. At each post the post master took the letters for his own district and gave the courier new mail to be delivered elsewhere. A new rider on a fresh horse then carried the letters to the next post.

Oliver Cromwell continued to develop the system, calling it the General Post Office. His first Postmaster General was none other than Wisbech's own John Thurloe, Cromwell's spymaster. He is believed to have used his position to open, decode and intercept letters, resealing them carefully so that no one suspected.

The cost of postage was calculated by the distance the letter was carried and the number of sheets of paper it contained. Envelopes were not used, as they would have counted as an extra sheet of paper and increased the cost.

Instead, letters were simply folded over, sealed with wax and stamped with the seal of the sender. It was the recipient, not the sender, however, who paid the postage, and the revenue went to the government.

In 1681, during the reign of Charles II, a former government clerk called Robert Murray introduced the Penny Post to London. His messengers called at coffee houses for letters and carried them across the city in a ten mile radius. Each letter cost a penny to send and the system worked very well. Before this, there had been no system for the carriage of post within the city; anyone wishing to send a message had had to pay private messengers. The Penny Post was therefore very popular and eventually became part of the General Post Office. Coaches gradually replaced mounted couriers and an increasing number of regular delivery routes were established across the country.

Another institution of the modern world, the Bank of England, was founded in 1694. Initially, it was created to manage the government's debts. War with France had resulted in a significant and expensive expansion of the Royal Navy, and the government used the Bank of England to finance ship building on credit.

From the shaping of central finance to the control of pay and conditions for agricultural workers, regulation was having an ever increasing effect on the working life of Britain. The work done by the least privileged members of society continued to be menial and hard, but unemployment was harder still.

Yet, however hard and badly paid the work, and however long the hours, the people of England still tried to find a little time for play.

Spinning Tops...and Bottoms; Play Time

The only free time for the vast majority of working people came on a Sunday. Even then, there was church to attend, so any leisure had to be fitted into Sunday afternoons.

The most popular English sports and pastimes had changed little from medieval times. Fishing supplemented the family diet while ensuring a few restful hours, but bowling, wrestling and football were preferable for the more energetic. Bowling was growing in popularity and bowling alleys and greens were appearing in towns and village ale houses all over the country. There is known to have been a bowling alley, as well as a tennis court, near Leverington in the 1570s.

Football, also known as camping, was a favourite sport for men and boys. On Sundays, men from two neighbouring villages would play against each other, using an inflated pig's bladder as a ball. There were no football pitches, no limit to the size of teams, and games could go on for hours. Players chased the ball along streets and across fields and play was very rough, resulting in a multitude of injuries. Despite this, football, especially at Shrovetide, had become a very popular English tradition.

But by far the most seriously practised sport, and not entirely by choice, was archery. Henry VIII needed to ensure that the country had enough trained archers in the event of war. By Act of Parliament, it was decreed that all men under the age of sixty, with the exception of clergymen and judges, should regularly practise their skills. Archery practice after church on Sundays was considered a man's patriotic duty, but it could still be fun. Alehouses overlooking the local butts did a good Sunday trade.

Children too young for serious sport might play leap frog, blind man's buff, or use rounded pebbles as marbles. The more fortunate might have wooden toys, such as spinning tops or dolls, made by an indulgent parent or servant.

Sports and pastimes played a significant part in the lives of wealthy Tudors. Jousting, hawking and hunting on horseback were popular with the upper classes who also shared a love of simpler pursuits with other classes. Even Henry VIII had a bowling alley at Hampton Court.

The young King Henry also loved tennis. The game he knew was an older form than that played today and is referred to now as 'real tennis'. It was played with balls of tightly packed wool which were bounced off the walls of specially built indoor courts.

More sedentary pastimes included dominoes, cards and 'shove-groat', later to be known as shove-halfpenny.

Dancing was very popular with the young, many of whom spent Sunday afternoons dancing to the music of pipers and drummers. Some of the fittest participated in Morris dancing and on May Day they danced around maypoles. King Henry himself loved to dance, especially the energetic 'tourdion', with its high leaps. The more formal and graceful 'basse dance' was also popular at court.

Page from a hand painted medieval choir book (with permission of the Wisbech and Fenland Museum)

The educated upper classes were expected to play a musical instrument, such as the virginal, a keyboard instrument rather like a small harpsichord which made a tinkling sound. Music was not just for the wealthy, though. Travelling musicians took their songs to towns and villages everywhere, playing flutes, lutes and viols.

The Tudor and Stuart periods were cruel times. People were used to harsh laws and the threat of savage punishment, so perhaps it isn't surprising that they considered cock fighting, bull and bear baiting to be acceptable forms of entertainment. These horrible spectacles were popular with many.

Theatre going was considerably less harmful. Morality plays had arrived from Europe in the 1490s and, as the same suggests, they carried a strong moral message usually developed from Bible stories. The players travelled in a wagon around the country, arriving in town market places, where they set up their stage on the wagon itself. One popular play was 'Everyman', an allegory of human life and death which personified virtues and vices. Plays were often performed by guild members, each guild choosing a play appropriate to their particular craft. For example, 'The Last Supper' was played by bakers, 'The Crucifixion' by nail-makers.

When players were invited to perform at court they had to take care. As the king aged, he became increasingly suspicious and fearful of sedition. He created a new post of Master of the Revels, an officer responsible for supervising all court entertainment and theatrical performances and for reporting any suspicious speech or behaviour.

Henry's reign saw a lot of religious conflict but also the development of art and fresh ideas. Sir Thomas More's 'Utopia', published in 1516, described a perfect form of government in which all men were equal, all religions were tolerated and men and women were educated together. Sir Thomas was sadly way ahead of his time.

He became one of the first patrons of a new German artist, Hans Holbein, who came to London in 1527. He impressed London society with the realism of his painting and was soon working for the king himself. His paintings of Henry and other members of the royal family remain as some of our most familiar images of that period.

Queen Elizabeth I shared her father's love of music, dance and his zest for life. This was the time of the English Renaissance, when art and culture reached new heights.

New musical compositions ranged from the sacred to the secular and, now that sheet music could be produced by the printing press, new compositions reached a wider audience. Some of the most popular composers of the time were William Byrd and John Dowland.

The queen played the lute and the virginal. It was a great time for music generally, favourite tunes of the day being played on recorders, bells and the viol (a six stringed instrument with a fretted fingerboard). There were also the bandore (an ancient banjo), the cithern (an early form of guitar), and the dulcimer. This was an ancestor of the piano on which the keys were struck, rather than plucked.

The theatre underwent a huge transformation during Elizabeth's reign. Morality plays had fallen out of favour after Henry VIII's Reformation and something was needed to fill the gap. New legislation of 1572 required all groups of players to be licensed and this led to the emergence of a new breed of professional players. The theatre was becoming very fashionable among the elite.

For the first time, in 1576 a permanent, purpose built theatre was constructed. The new building, constructed in Shoreditch by the actor and manager James Burbage, was simply called 'The Theatre'. Its polygonal wooden auditorium had three covered galleries surrounding an open air cobbled area in front of the stage. For a penny, a theatre goer could watch the performance from this unsheltered area, but tuppence paid for standing room in one of the galleries. An extra penny lent them a stool to sit on.

The first performances staged by the Earl of Leicester's Men, actors under the patronage of the Queen's favourite, Robert Dudley, were very popular. They were so successful, in fact, that another theatre, the Curtain, was soon built nearby.

Richard Burbage, the son of James, later became the leading actor in another troupe, the Lord Chamberlain's Men. Another principal actor in this company was William Shakespeare.

The Lord Chamberlain's Men moved to a newly constructed theatre, the Globe on London's south bank, and their popularity grew. During the Christmas of 1594, they performed at court for Queen Elizabeth herself. Richard Burbage and William Shakespeare were among the players on this occasion and they must have made a good impression because it turned out to be the first of several such performances.

London's new Globe Theatre in Southwark

Costumes and sets became ever more elaborate and colourful, but only men and boys were allowed on stage, so the audience had to use a bit of imagination.

The plays written by William Shakespeare were enormously popular and he wrote prolifically. To express his characters' feelings and to describe situations, he invented new words, many of which were absorbed into the English language. For example, nouns such as 'moonbeam' and 'bedroom' had not previously been used.

Another popular playwright was Christopher Marlowe, best remembered for works like 'Doctor Faustus' and 'The Jew of Malta'.

The creation of theatres on the outskirts of London did not end the tradition of travelling theatrical troupes. Actors continued to stage their plays in the galleried courtyards of inns, as well as the great halls of large houses, palaces and colleges.

By 1600 there were five theatres in the capital and in 1608 a new type of playhouse was backed by Richard Burbage. This was an indoor theatre at Blackfriars, a more practical venue for the winter season than open air buildings. Because of the number of candles it took to light it, it was more expensive both to run and to attend, but it was more intimate. Shakespeare wrote new plays, such as 'The Winter's Tale' and 'The Tempest', to make the most of its darker scenic effects.

Other writers were also well received at the time. In 1596 the poet Edmund Spenser published 'The Faerie Queene'. The poem celebrated the chivalric virtues of the past and referred to Elizabeth I, the virgin queen, as 'Gloriana'. As a result, despite the queen being by then in her sixties, the Gloriana cult really took off. Although she had to use wigs and heavy make-up to give the illusion of youth, her portraits continued to show her as beautiful and strong. Under her leadership, England had defeated the Armada and her explorers continued to bring back discoveries and tales from the far reaches of the globe. The English were very proud of it.

Elizabeth continued the tradition of the monarch's summer progress around the country. She travelled with her court, staying for weeks at a time in the homes of her nobles. Many were keen to entertain her and to gain royal favour, but such hospitality came at enormous expense. In July 1575 she visited Robert Dudley, the Earl of Leicester, at Kenilworth Castle. She stayed for several weeks and was lavishly entertained with sumptuous banquets, masques, plays, fireworks, hunting, music and dancing. There was also, of course, bear-baiting.

These poor animals were, however, to have some small respite under Elizabeth's successor, James I.

James inherited a kingdom which was divided in its beliefs. The Puritans, who were voicing their opinions more and more, loudly condemned the frivolity they saw around them.

The king, who was more than capable of enjoying life, displayed his more serious side with the publication of a new translation of the Bible. This, the King James Bible of 1611, was the third translation since Henry VIII's time and remains the authorised version to this day.

There were constant disputes between the Puritans and the more fun-loving sectors of society. The Puritans believed that Sundays should be kept free of both work and levity, while others, for whom Sunday was usually their only day off, wanted to enjoy themselves after church.

With the issue of the 'King James' Book of Sports' in 1618, the king attempted to establish a compromise between the two factions. His ruling allowed Puritans to stay true to their beliefs, so long as they refrained from trying to coerce others. Those who wanted to, were free to enjoy themselves after church on Sundays and Holy Days, but the activities they were permitted to indulge in were limited. Archery, dancing, leaping and vaulting were allowed. Even the seasonal traditions so disdained by the Puritans, such as maypole and Morris dancing, were considered harmless and allowed to continue. Bloodthirsty and cruel sports, however, such as bull and bear-baiting, were prohibited on Sundays. At least this gave the poor creatures one day off.

The national love of sport could be seen everywhere. The Cotswold Games of 1612 included football, quoits, wrestling, shin-kicking, dancing, running races, horse racing, bowls and skittles. There were even events for the less athletic, such as shove-groat and chess.

The Scottish game of golf was rapidly becoming popular all over the country and would gradually evolve into the game we know today.

Meanwhile, a completely different sort of entertainment was gaining favour with the wealthy. The idea of the London Season was established between 1590 and 1620. During the winter, wealthy families began to escape the mud of the countryside and move to the capital to enjoy its many pleasures. The London theatre was one of those pleasures, with playwrights such as Ben Jonson and John Webster following on from Shakespeare. Webster's 'The Duchess of Malfi' was a great favourite.

The Protectorate is remembered for its suppression of entertainment, rather than for its promotion. Feasting and the decoration of homes at Christmas, as well as springtime maypoles and other seasonal celebrations, were prohibited. In 1642 the theatres were closed and any actors found performing in secret were arrested.

Not every pastime was banned, of course. Books such as Izaak Walton's 'The Compleat Angler' were unlikely to attract criticism. Published in 1653, it was a mixture of technical instruction, humour and contemplation.

The restoration of the monarchy in 1660 brought a great outpouring of relief. Theatres re-opened and were packed nightly with enthusiastic Londoners. Charles II himself loved the theatre and one of his first actions as king was to allow women to appear on stage. The diarist Samuel Pepys wrote on the third of January 1661 about going to see the play 'Beggar's Bush' and seeing women act on stage for the first time.

In 1663 the Theatre Royal was opened in Drury Lane. As well as sophisticated scenery, it had a proscenium arch in front of the curtain which separated the action on stage from the audience. The proscenium arch was to become a familiar feature of theatres.

The appearance of women on stage made the theatre even more appealing. Young actresses like Nell Gwyn and Moll Davis enjoyed huge popularity, as did the writer Aphra Behn. She was one of the first women to earn a living from producing poetry, fiction and stage plays.

Another passion of the king's was horse racing, which during his reign became known as the Sport of Kings. Horse race meetings were held at Newmarket, which has maintained the tradition ever since.

The mood immediately following the restoration was one of greater freedom, but there were some who thought things had gone too far. The king was known for his scandalous parties, and bawdy behaviour in general was increasingly tolerated. Playwrights such as William Congreve and John Dryden were criticised by people of a more sober disposition for the use of swearing and blasphemy in their plays.

Perhaps what sums up the mood of the times more than anything, was a new establishment called the Farting Club, founded in a public house in Grub Street, Cripplegate. No prizes for guessing what went on there! It is said that little boys used to listen at the club's windows then run up and down the street making raspberry noises with their armpits. Some things never change.

The freezing winters of that time produced conditions so severe in 1684 that even the Thames froze. For a month, the ice was so thick that a Frost Fair was held on the river and traders set up booths to sell their wares. Londoners, keen to forget the miserable cold for a while, flocked there to be entertained by sword swallowing, puppet shows, music and dancing, as well as the inevitable bear-baiting. Incredibly, the thickness of the ice even allowed horse racing to take place. One of the booths contained a real novelty, a printing press which printed the customer's name on to small visiting cards.

In the early 1700s, the idea of fashionable seasons away from home was developed further. The city of Bath was fast becoming the place to be seen for English and Welsh gentry. A summer season was being established for the wealthy who visited to sample the healthy benefits of the local spring water. Assembly rooms were built for their entertainment, and to make the Bath season suitable for the highest ranking individuals, a strict code of conduct and dress was imposed.

A usual Bath day began with the morning at the baths followed by a visit to the pump room to exchange gossip. In the afternoon, men might visit a coffee house while women gathered in private houses or walked in the countryside. Evenings were spent in private dining, card playing, dancing or a trip to the theatre.

This tradition would grow in popularity throughout the Georgian period to come. New tastes were steadily replacing Tudor and Stuart customs and were just some of the signs that Great Britain was ready to embrace the future.

But there was more going on than mere entertainment. The Tudor and Stuart periods were times of significant progress, both in thinking and education, so it is time to take a look.

A Headless Man on the Moon; Thinking and Learning

The Tudors came to prominence at about the same time as the printed word.

When, in 1476, William Caxton set up his first printing press near the Westminster Abbey chapter house, he set in motion a great surge in communication and the spread of knowledge. Despite all the advances in technology since then, more than five hundred years later his work continues to benefit us all.

William Caxton had learned the art of printing with movable type in Cologne. The first book to be printed there is thought to have been the Gutenberg Bible in 1455. Having set up his London press, he began by setting into print an old favourite, Chaucer's 'Canterbury Tales'. It sold so well that Caxton produced a second edition, this time with woodcut illustrations. Sir Thomas Malory's 'Morte d'Arthur' followed soon afterwards.

The printing press led to the publication of many new works. One author to take advantage of the new technology was a Wisbech man, Richard Herlock. In 1522 he published a grammar book, 'The English ABC', dedicating it to Thomas Goodrich, the Bishop of Ely and

Chancellor of England. At the time, only works of a religious or highly intellectual nature were deemed worthy to be dedicated to such an elevated person and Richard Herlock's book had what was considered to be a 'low title'. Fortunately, the bishop received it with good grace, seeing its merits as a teaching aid. Such books were greatly needed. The standard of education was generally very poor at that time and few members of the lower classes were able to read or write.

Before the printed word, the spread of knowledge had relied greatly on the hand written manuscripts produced in the monasteries. Often richly illustrated, hundreds of these precious manuscripts were burned in acts of vandalism by the king's men in the name of Reform.

End page from a medieval manuscript from the collection at Wisbech and Fenland Museum (with permission of the museum)

The dissolution of the monasteries created voids in just about every walk of life. Monks had carried out so many tasks and their sudden absence created a need for new administrators and professionals to do their old jobs. Clerks, book keepers and estate managers were much in demand and there was more need than ever for boys to be well educated.

A boy's chances of receiving a good education depended hugely on the class he was born into. The sons of the gentry and aristocracy usually began their schooling with private tutors at home, going on to boarding school later. Tutored in the classical Greek and Latin deemed essential for gentlemen, they were expected to study hard. Their school days were long, usually from 6am to 5.30pm, six days a week.

After boarding school, it was normal for young gentlemen to attend one of the growing number of universities. There they might meet the sons of middle class merchants who were preparing for careers in teaching, law, medicine or the Church. By the end of the Tudor period there were nine universities in England.

Less advantaged boys might attend grammar school from the age of seven, but this certainly wasn't for everyone. There were still fees to be paid so this kind of education was beyond the reach of most families.

Early Tudor girls, however well bred, did not attend school. The emphasis of their education was on learning to be good, obedient wives who could cook, sew and grow vegetables. Even the daughters of wealthy families received only a basic education, staying at home to be taught to read and write by tutors.

However, thanks to influential thinkers like Sir Thomas More and the Dutch scholar Erasmus, new views on the education of women were emerging. Queen Elizabeth, when she came to the throne, was a further good influence. She was well educated herself and many upper and middle class families were keen to follow her example, providing a better education for their daughters. Even the better placed lower classes were influenced by this wave of new thinking. Some of their daughters were sent to parish schools to learn how to keep accounts for the family business.

One method for teaching children to read used a wooden board and letters written on slips of paper. The paper letters were arranged on the board to form the alphabet or new words and a sheet of transparent horn kept them in place. Children learned by chanting the alphabet as the tutor pointed to each letter. Traditionally, the first set of words a child learned to read was the Lord's Prayer.

Children whose families could afford it were taught to write with quills fashioned from goose, swan or raven feathers. The pens were dipped in ink and scratched across the paper. Poorer students, though, were more likely to write on a slate or even to trace letters in sand.

The alphabet differed only slightly from that used today. The modern lower case r was used for the letter c, and the letter s had three different forms, depending on where it occurred in a word.

King Edward VI, despite his youth and short reign, founded twenty-six new grammar schools in England. He had inherited the throne in 1547, when the vast majority of his subjects were illiterate, and he was determined to improve the situation. As well as opening new schools, he re-founded old establishments which had been run by churches and religious guilds, as in Wisbech. The funding for these schools came mostly through endowments from former chantry lands seized by the crown.

One of today's oldest surviving English boarding schools was founded by Edward. He wanted to do something for the huge number of orphans who were living in poverty on London streets and his new Christ's Hospital went some way towards alleviating the problem. Built on the site of a dissolved Franciscan priory in Newgate Street, the hospital, which was more of a boarding school in today's terms, admitted three hundred and eighty poor children when it first opened in 1553. The number of students rapidly increased over the years and, unusually for the times, girls as well as boys were accepted. Students were provided with regular meals, uniforms, lodgings and education. To prepare them for a successful working life, they were taught crafts such as spinning and weaving, as well as to read and write. Their uniform of a long blue coat and breeches with yellow stockings is still worn with pride today by the school's pupils.

Queen Elizabeth continued her brother's work by encouraging the creation of new grammar schools, but because the state coffers were so frequently empty during her reign, no funding was provided and many schools had to rely on charitable donations.

Tudor schools were simple in construction. A school room, chapel and a house for the master were usually all that was considered necessary.

Queen Elizabeth's reign saw not only the flourishing of art, music and literature, but also considerable progress in medicine and science.

One of the most learned yet controversial figures of the time was John Dee. He was a mathematician, astronomer and astrologer who was also drawn to the occult. At his home in Mortlake (then in Surrey) he had the largest personal library in England, housing books on every subject that fascinated him. Among them were the works of polish born Nicolas Copernicus.

At a time when many still believed the earth to be at the centre of the universe, John Dee reinforced Copernicus' theory that the earth and other planets revolved around the sun. Such outrageous claims did not endear him to many, but it was his interest in astrology and the occult which really landed him in trouble. During the reign of Queen Mary, he had been accused of trying to kill the queen through sorcery. Fortunately, he survived his ordeal to become Queen Elizabeth's personal astronomer.

Well-to-do Elizabethan families keen to boost their sons' education sent them abroad to enrich their learning. France and Italy were the usual destinations, while the youth of Europe explored London, Cambridge and Oxford. English travellers didn't always make the most of the culture available to them, however. Suspicions about how some of them spent their time grew through the publication in Liège of a new phrasebook. The book devoted several pages to guidance on how to seduce a chamber maid in seven different languages.

Yet, despite a few wasted opportunities, the level of education in England was gradually improving. At the beginning of the Tudor period only five percent of men and one percent of women were thought to have been able to read and write. By 1640, it was estimated that around half the population of London and a third of rural men were literate. About two and a half percent of seventeen year old boys were attending university.

Progress in the education of women was far slower. It was still generally believed that teaching them anything more than housekeeping was a waste of time. There were some, however, who tried to improve matters. In 1616 Mary Ward, an English Catholic, left her homeland, where

Catholics faced persecution, to set up schools for women in France. Despite a barrage of criticism that she was over educating her pupils, she was determined to give them a proper start in life. In her schools at St Omer and Liège girls were taught Greek, Latin, French, maths and astronomy.

The 1600s, despite the horrors of civil war, were times of significant research and scientific progress.

In agriculture, a new publication of 1601 recommended the sowing of seeds in regular rows of holes in the soil. The old tradition of broadcasting seeds from a basket was declared to be inefficient. It would still be some time before the seed drill was invented to make the new method easier, but it was still a breakthrough.

Scientists such as Thomas Harriot and Sir William Lower were making new discoveries in the field of astronomy. Harriot, who had been mathematics tutor to Sir Walter Raleigh, was the first Englishman to observe sunspots through his telescope. In 1610, he recorded more than a hundred sunspot observations in a month, and using this information, was able to measure the sun's axial rotation. With Lower, he looked at the moons of Jupiter and observed our own moon. Some of Lower's observations were quite fanciful. He likened what he saw to a tart his cook had made and described one of the shapes as like a headless man on the moon.

By 1666 even amateur enthusiasts were using telescopes. In his diary, Samuel Pepys described how he took a 'twelve foot glass' to the roof of his house to look at the moon, Saturn and Jupiter. Sadly, cloudy skies made the experience a bit disappointing for him.

An ingenious breakthrough in mathematics occurred in 1614 when John Napier of Merchiston, Edinburgh invented a new calculating device. Later known as Napier's Bones, it consisted of a wooden frame containing a number of rods marked with series of numbers. By placing the rods in certain ways within the frame, division and multiplication could be done with ease. More advanced use of the rods could even calculate square roots.

Greater understanding of human biology was achieved by William Harvey. Through experimentation, he worked out how blood was pumped by the heart around the body. He was so respected for his work that he became royal physician to James I.

One of his later discoveries was how an embryo developed. He realised that a baby was first formed as an egg, rather than, as had been assumed before, as a fully formed tiny person which grew in the womb. What Harvey couldn't work out was how the egg itself was formed. Such knowledge would only come with the much later invention of the microscope.

Meanwhile, cartographers were creating far more accurate maps than before. During the late 1500s and early 1600s, Suffolk man Radulph Agas created a number of detailed maps of the East of England, all of which showed north to the right hand side of the page. Among them were useful maps of the Fens.

In 1610, a new book of maps of England and Wales was published by the cartographer and historian John Speed. His atlas with the grand title, 'Theatre of the Empire of Great Britain' contained his first set of individual county maps and was very well received.

John Ogilby, as mentioned earlier, produced a series of useful maps in 1675. His strip maps of every major route in England, Scotland and Wales enabled a stranger for the first time to travel from Land's End to John o' Groats without having to employ a guide. John Ogilby's atlas was modestly entitled 'English Itinery. A Book of Roads.'

Other publications were intended for moral guidance. Richard Brathwaite's guide to etiquette, 'The English Gentlewoman' promoted modesty, chastity and obedience as the virtues of a good gentlewoman.

A different sort of publication altogether expressed the strong political and religious feelings which surfaced during the civil war and the Protectorate. In 1652 Sir Edward Peyton wrote the innocent sounding 'The Divine Catastrophe of the Kingly Family of the House of Stuarts'.

At first glance, it looked like a lament following the regicide of King Charles I. The work, however, was written by a member of an extreme Puritan sect called the Fifth Monarchists. As such, Sir Edward believed in the prophecy of the Book of Daniel which said that four ancient monarchies would precede the return of Jesus as king. Counting Babylon, Persia, Macedonia and Rome as the four, the Fifth Monarchists saw the death of King Charles as a sign that the prophecy was about to be fulfilled, and eagerly awaited the arrival of King Jesus. At any other time, such dangerous writing would have meant death for the author, but such opinions were tolerated during the Protectorate.

Archaeology had never aroused much curiosity in the English, but towards the end of the seventeenth century a few people were showing interest. The antiquarian, John Aubrey, became fascinated with the ancient standing stones of Stonehenge and Avebury, believing them once to have been druid temples. This new insight, about what had always been disregarded as a load of old rocks, was laughed at by many, but at least it was a start.

This was also a time of greater understanding of physics. In 1687 Isaac Newton, the Cambridge professor, mathematician and physicist, shared his research with the wider world in his book 'Principia Mathematica'. In this important book he explained the effect of gravity on the earth, and we've never looked back.

In 1699, the Society for Promoting Christian Knowledge provided a different kind of boost to education. Spurred on by the ever increasing levels of lawlessness in London and the unprecedented rise in robberies and murders, the society wanted to offer poor children a brighter future. They opened a number of schools in the city where disadvantaged children were taught the catechism, as well as to read and write.

While education shaped the way we thought, other factors influenced the way we behaved. Social graces were every bit as important as learning when it came to getting on in life.

The Doffing of Caps; Social Graces and Society

England took a long time to recover from the effects of plague and war which had dominated the fourteenth and fifteenth centuries. The English population had fallen to less than three million and many families had been wiped out altogether. Some of them had aristocratic roots traceable back to the Normans.

There was no shortage of newly wealthy families in early Tudor England to take their place, but money alone was not enough to qualify their offspring to marry into the upper orders. They needed to be accepted by what was left of the old nobility and the established merchant classes.

Publications known as courtesy books were useful in this regard. These books explained the etiquette of the day in an attempt to help ambitious families avoid embarrassment in their social climbing.

One of the most important topics covered by the books was table manners. At the table, it was stressed, it was important to allow one's superiors to serve themselves first from the communal dishes. The wiping of noses on the table cloth was strongly discouraged, as was spitting, scratching oneself, telling dirty jokes and breaking wind.

Some upper class practices, however, were not worthy of imitation. In 1496 the Venetian ambassador wrote home about the way in which the English upper classes treated their offspring. It was quite normal at that time for children from the age of seven to be sent to live in the homes of other families. This was not as honoured guests, though, but as servants. To teach them manners and respect for their elders, they were fed the coarsest bread and treated like any other domestic servant. Meanwhile, their parents took in children from other families, also as servants. In this way, high-born families were always served by strangers' children, carefully avoiding any danger of sentimentality getting in the way.

Unsurprisingly, few of these children ever went back home. After seven to nine years of servitude, boys tended to marry and girls often remained with their patrons.

Thankfully, this practice gradually died out and upper class children were allowed to remain at home to be versed in etiquette. From early childhood they were taught perfect posture. Boys walked with a swagger, thrusting their hips forward, and were encouraged to be bold and assertive. In contrast, a ploughman, who spent his life working in the fields, walked with a slow, plodding gait. It was easy to spot a person's origins by the way they moved.

There was a completely different set of expectations for girls. From childhood they were taught to be mild mannered and timid.

Both boys and girls were expected to show deference to adults, even to those of lower social standing. They learned to bow and curtsey as soon as they were old enough to do so. Young men were taught to execute a formal bow, dropping to one knee. Young ladies learned to curtsey while keeping their head perfectly erect and their back straight, lowering their eyes. Their arms were kept to the sides, palms upwards. Even the very young were expected to give some semblance of a polite greeting; a boy doffed his cap while a girl gave a little bob of a curtsey.

At the opposite end of the social scale existed the homeless and others who lived in poverty. Though the problem had been made so much worse by Henry VIII's dissolution of the monasteries, he did practically nothing to help. His son, Edward VI, introduced laws aimed more at punishing the most unfortunate victims of poverty than at helping them. His laws required vagabonds found outside their own parishes to be sent home. If they refused, they were whipped and branded with a V. However harsh, this was at least a slight improvement on earlier laws which had punished the troublesome homeless with death.

Such an unsympathetic stance did nothing to alleviate the problem. By Queen Elizabeth's time, the number of beggars, criminals and vagabonds was so large that many had set up camps on the outskirts of towns. Their lawlessness terrified the inhabitants and it was most likely this which in 1567 finally prompted parliament to pass a bill providing statutory relief for the poor.

Under the new Poor Law, the parish was made responsible for the relief of its poorest members. It had to find employment and provide tools for those who were willing and able to work. The parish was also responsible for supporting the aged and handicapped, allowing them to remain in their own homes. The law was still tough on individuals who refused to work, branding, whipping and sending them back to their own parishes. Houses of correction were established, where they were sent to work.

Poor box dated 1639 in the parish church of Walpole St Peter (with permission of the parish church)

Women's rights had improved very little since the medieval age. They were still considered inferior to men, believed to have been created to serve and obey them. It was rare for the daughters of landed families to inherit property and it only occurred where there were no living male relatives. On marriage, any property belonging to the wife instantly became part of her husband's estate.

Even so, English women probably had a better deal than most. Thomas Platter, a Swiss born traveller and diarist, made some interesting observations about English women during a visit here in 1599. Having commented on how fair and pretty they were, he noticed that they enjoyed more liberty than in other countries. He observed how freely they visited inns and taverns, just like men, and how they strolled around in attractive clothes with starched ruffs.

These minor advances in female freedom were not pleasing to everyone. In 1616 a real charmer by the name of Joseph Swetman published a pamphlet entitled 'An Arraignment of Lewd, Idle, Forward and Inconstant Women'. His main message was that women sprang from the devil, that they were born subordinate to men and should be ruled by them. He recommended regular wife-beating to maintain the correct patriarchal order. His pamphlet was enormously popular, though probably only with men.

Although by the beginning of the seventeenth century population figures had begun to recover from their early Tudor low, the birth rate had started to fall again. Social behaviour had a lot to do with this, in that marriage was taking place later. Although legally girls could marry from the age of twelve and boys from fourteen, they were doing so far less often. Children of poorer families were going into long term domestic service and sending money home to help their parents. As servants living in their employer's home, their wages were small, slowing down their ability to save for marriage.

Even the middle and upper classes were marrying later. Improved standards of education and training meant that university or apprenticeships had to be finished before marriage could be considered.

Marriage was taking place more now in the mid twenties than in the teens. Only the nobility kept to the old tradition, arranging early marriages for their children in order to secure the future for their titles, wealth and estates.

The perils of childbirth did not help population figures. As mentioned earlier, death of the mother or child was common and only about half of the babies who made it into the world survived to the age of five. Adults who lived beyond fifty were considered fortunate.

Fewer mouths to feed meant that agriculture was better able to keep up and there was more food to go round. Famine occurred less often, but inevitably there were still bad harvests. At such times, the price of grain rose faster than wages, leading to hunger for many. By 1640, this cycle of poor harvests and famine finally urged the government to intervene. They began to regulate the storage of grain in good years, creating a surplus to help in lean years. It was no guarantee against hunger, but it was something.

The religious upheaval that had begun with King Henry's Reforms had led to the formation of many religious sects. Conflicting views and prejudices created an unhealthy climate in which some members of society came under scrutiny. In 1612 a book called 'The Wonderful Discovery of Witches in the County of Lancashire' was published. It was a fanciful description of the supposed misdeeds of witches and led to a dangerous fascination with them.

Any poor woman living alone, or anyone who didn't fit in or was disliked, could easily fall under suspicion of witchcraft. Once a woman was accused, a charge of witchcraft was almost impossible to disprove. Most of the cases that went to court resulted in a guilty verdict and death by hanging. The most zealous witch finder was Matthew Hopkins, who travelled around East Anglia during the early civil war years. He charged the authorities a fee for every witch he identified, giving him the perfect incentive to find as many as possible. In the three years following 1644 he is thought to have caused the death of at least three hundred women.

Life was not improving for English Catholics either. After a hundred and fifty years of persecution, the Act of Settlement of 1704 made their future even less certain. The Act was passed during the reign of the Protestant William of Orange and ensured that never again could a Catholic inherit the throne.

Other legislation prevented them from leasing land for more than thirty-one years. They could no longer inherit land from a Protestant or acquire land through marriage. On their death, their property had to be divided between their sons, but if any of their sons became Protestants, they could inherit the entire estate. Catholics were forbidden to educate their children abroad, where establishments like Mary Ward's girls' schools in France would have nourished their beliefs. On top of all this, all Catholics had to take an oath of allegiance before voting in elections or holding public office.

Life in Stuart England, therefore, continued to be tough for anyone who didn't fit in. For those who did, for the Protestant gentry, merchants and professionals, life could be very pleasant. By the end of the seventeenth century, the upper classes and professional middle classes were co-existing in a genial way. For them, social etiquette was highly valued. Qualities such as civility and the use of the correct form of address were seen as the marks of a respectable person.

Newspapers such as the Daily Courant and the London Gazette kept them up to date with business and politics, while the Tatler, first published in 1709, reported the latest coffee house gossip.

And when the people of Stuart England addressed each other it was in their own regional dialects. King James I had made sure of that.

When King James VI of Scotland first came south to claim the English throne he was ridiculed for his Scottish brogue. He was considered uncouth by the English, even though his accent, like English, was one of many derived from German dialects brought here by sixth century invaders. Despite this history, there was an attempt to introduce a form of standardised English in Edinburgh. It did not work. The Scottish aristocracy and gentry persisted in the use of Lowland Scots accents, setting a precedent which ensured the survival of the many diverse accents and dialects of England, Scotland, Wales and Ireland.

A rigid class system was still in place by the end of the Stuart period. The nobility continued to enjoy life at the top, second only to the king himself. Beneath them were the well established merchants and the gentry, some of whom were the squires of rural communities. The yeomen occupied the rung beneath them on the social scale, the husbandmen below them. At the bottom were the cottagers, the poorest folk for whom life was generally the toughest.

With this structure firmly in place and the horrors of civil war safely behind them, the English had reached a new level of stability. It was a far cry from the medieval world inherited by Henry VII, the first of the Tudors.

From life in the shadow of the monasteries, through dissolution, disease, civil war and prejudice, Great Britain had emerged into something like a modern state. With its Reformed Church, its rebuilt capital, scientific progress and global exploration, the country was poised on the threshold of a new period of discovery.

As for the people of the Fens, they were still trying to come to terms with their newly drained landscape. Many were struggling to find their way, while others were adapting and succeeding.

And the town of Wisbech, with its thriving port and market, had seen off plague, fires, Cromwell and more flooding than it could possibly remember. Wisbech was steadily growing, primed and ready like the rest of the country for a new age; the time of the Georgians.

Part of Bishop Alcock's 15th century palace in Ely

AFTERWORD AND THANKS

Trying to put together any sort of history book involves, of course, many long hours of reading through all sorts of material. Very often, different sources contradict each other, making a lot of puzzle solving necessary.

Equally frustrating is all the missing information. Key events, locations of buildings and outcomes of situations so often seem to have been left unrecorded, leaving modern researchers to wonder, perhaps to guess.

One example of this is the lack of an exact date for when the tower of St Peter's Church collapsed. It is generally believed to have occurred around 1500 and while some sources allude to it happening at night, others talk about it being in stormy weather. Whatever the truth, it is likely that centuries of flooding and the tower's close proximity to the old castle dyke weakened its foundations. The version involving a storm makes sense too; heavy rainfall, coupled with a strong wind, could well have been the last straw for the ancient tower.

Wisbech is such an interesting town. I know I keep saying it, but quite apart from its heritage and multiple layers of history, it is home to many knowledgeable and generous people who have kindly shared their research and detective work with me. I am very grateful to the following people and places for their help and advice.

Andy Ketley
Bridget Holmes
Cromwell's House Museum, Ely
Dr Eric Somerville
Dr Michael Gilbert
Edward Sandall

Michelle Lawes
Robert Bell and Geoff Hill of Wisbech and Fenland Museum
The Fenland Archaeological Society
The National Trust Photo Library
The National Trust's Peckover House
The National Trust's Ramsey Abbey Gatehouse
The Parish Church of St Peter and St Paul
The Parish Church of Walpole St Peter
The Wisbech Society
Wisbech Library

And then, when all the information is gathered and I've spent another few months in shaping the text into something readable, my ever patient husband, Tony, steps in with his proof-reading and the creation of maps and illustrations. I give him my heartfelt thanks.

APPENDIX

Pre-decimal currency:

£1 = 20 shillings (1 shilling equates to 5 new pence)
1 shilling = 12 old pence (12d).
A groat was worth four old pence (4d).
Pennies were divided into half pennies and farthings (quarter pennies).

BIBLIOGRAPHY

'A Companion to Local History Research' John Campbell-Kease
'A Fenland Country Christmas' Edward Storey
'A History of the County of Cambridgeshire and the Isle of Ely Vol 4'
'A Tour through the Whole Island of Great Britain' Daniel Defoe
'An Autobiography of an Elizabethan; William Weston', translated by Philip Caraman
'An Historical Account of the Ancient Town and Port of Wisbech in the Isle' William Watson
'Britain in Tudor Times' Fiona Macdonald
'Chronicles of Britain and Ireland' edited by Henrietta Heald
'Complete Herbal' Nicholas Culpeper
Court Rolls of Ramsey, Hepmangrove and Bury 1268 to 1600
'Cromwell' Antonia Fraser
Domestic Series of the State Papers
'Everyday Life – Focus on Tudor Life' Liz Gogerly
'Fen, Fire and Flood' Edward Storey
'Fenland, a landscape Made by Man' Peter Hewitt
'Fenland Notes and Queries' edited by Bernard Saunders
'History of Wisbech and Neighbourhood' R J Gardiner
'History, Gazetteer and Directory of Cambridgeshire 1851' Robert Gardner
'How to be a Tudor' Ruth Goodman
Peterborough Feoffees' Books 1614 onwards
'Prisoners of the Fens' Trevor Bevis
'Rich and Poor in Tudor Times' Peter D Riley
'Samuel Pepys, the Unequalled Self' Claire Tomalin
The British Postal Museum and Archive
'The Building of England' Simon Thurley
The Diary of Samuel Pepys

'The Draining of the Fens' Trevor Bevis
'The Historie of Great Britain' John Speed 1632
'The Local Historian's Encyclopaedia' John Richardson
'The Story of the Fens' Valerie Gerrard
'Wisbech in the Episcopal Registers' GMG Woodgate

INDEX OF NAMES AND PLACES
(except Wisbech itself)

Adventurers, 112, 116, 127, 129, 130
Anglesey Abbey, 40
Barton, 64, 74-77, 79, 93, 94, 174
Baskerville, Thomas, 254
Bedford Level Commission, 130, 131, 151
Bishop Alcock, 9, 28, 245
Bishop Cox, 60, 86
Bishop Goodrich, 27, 37, 40, 50
Bishop Morton, 7- 9
Black Bull Inn, 133
Butchers' Arms Inn, 72
Carlton, George 66, 67
Crabbe Marsh, 7, 64, 93
Cromwell, Oliver, 39, 117, 118, 122, 124, 127, 137, 193, 215
Cromwell, Thomas, 33, 35, 39, 42, 165
Crowland Abbey, 36, 70, 142
Crying Stone, 146
Deadman's Lane, 11, 74, 136
Defoe, Daniel, 152, 162, 249

Denny Abbey, 39
Elm, 2, 13, 14, 25, 50, 66, 69, 93, 108, 109, 119, 126, 137, 139, 157
Ely, 3, 7, 8, 9, 16, 23, 27, 33, 37, 38, 40, 45, 47, 50, 51, 54, 55, 60, 67, 83, 86, 95, 98, 99, 108, 117, 118, 119, 120, 121, 124, 126, 130, 134, 140, 147, 152, 153, 159, 228, 245, 246, 249
Emneth, 13, 27, 50, 69, 109, 119
Fen Tigers, 3, 128, 152
Fiennes, Celia, 158, 159
Gigg's Drove, 64
Gorefield, 13
Guild of the Holy Trinity, 5, 16, 17, 18, 19, 23, 26, 27, 41, 47, 48
Guyhirn, 7, 8, 15, 64, 65, 67, 73, 75, 93, 101, 102, 104, 109, 113, 115, 128, 130, 157
Hobhouse, 65, 66
Horseshoe, 64, 101, 117
King's Hall, 3, 93, 94, 174

251

Leverington, 2, 12, 13, 16, 23, 25, 50, 63, 64, 66, 72, 81, 101, 109, 137, 157, 217
Meadowgate Lane, 27
Morton's Leam, 7, 15, 102, 104, 128, 130, 149
Newton in the Isle, 13, 25, 29, 50, 66
Old Market, 11, 12, 63, 68, 74, 80, 99, 136, 145, 146, 155, 163
Outwell, 7, 15, 30, 49, 54, 69, 100, 113, 126, 139, 157
Parson Drove, 13, 28, 64, 65, 72, 154, 157
Peckover House, 3, 12, 94, 132, 135, 157, 174, 247
Pickards Lane, 145
Ramsey, 15, 22, 23, 31, 32, 33, 38, 39, 80, 127, 130, 149, 247, 249
Rose and Crown, 10, 145, 156, 162
Sandyland, 12, 49, 131, 145
Ship Lane, 11, 51, 74, 109, 133, 138, 148
Southwell family, 141
Spittal Cross, 69
Stuart, Jane, 155, 157
Sutton St Edmunds, 60, 61
Thurloe, John, 124, 128, 129, 135-141, 215
Timber Market, 7, 13, 49, 73, 74, 93, 172
Tydd Gote, 64
Tydd St Giles, 7, 13, 25, 29, 100, 102, 103, 157, 203
Ugg Mere, 22
Upwell, 7, 25, 49, 54, 55, 69, 81, 126, 127, 139, 157
Well Stream, 2, 7, 11, 13, 69, 93, 136
West Walton, 50
Whittlesey Mere, 22, 67, 113, 159
Wisbech Castle, 8, 55, 66, 83, 84, 85, 86, 95, 97, 135, 136
Wisbech Grammar School, 109, 133
Wisbech Stirs, 89
Wisbech Town Bridge, 9, 11, 68-69, 115, 131

Lightning Source UK Ltd.
Milton Keynes UK
UKHW011356150419
341049UK00001B/173/P